T0358426

GARLAND STUDIES ON

INDUSTRIAL PRODUCTIVITY

edited by

STUART BRUCHEY
ALLAN NEVINS PROFESSOR EMERITUS
COLUMBIA UNIVERSITY

TECHNOLOGICAL INNOVATION, INDUSTRIAL EVOLUTION, AND ECONOMIC GROWTH

SANJAYA PANTH

Routledge
Taylor & Francis Group
New York   London

First published by Garland Publishing, Inc.

This edition published 2013 by Routledge

Routledge
Taylor & Francis Group
711 Third Avenue
New York, NY 10017

Routledge
Taylor & Francis Group
2 Park Square, Milton Park
Abingdon, Oxon, OX14 4RN

Library of Congress Cataloging-in-Publication Data

Panth, Sanjaya.
Technological innovation, industrial evolution, and economic growth / Sanjaya Panth.
p.   cm. — (Garland studies on industrial productivity)
Includes bibliographical references and index.
ISBN 0-8153-2784-6 (alk. paper)
1. Technological innovations—Economic aspects.
2. Research, Industrial. 3. Economic development. I. Title.
II. Series.
HC79.T4P36 1997
38'.064—dc21   97-22274

To my father, Sachit Prashad Panth

Contents

Figures

Introduction

This book investigates the determinants of technological change and the role played by such change in the process of economic growth. The factors influencing the extent and dissemination of technological progress at the firm, industrial and societal levels are identified and the impact on the rate of economic growth of these factors is studied. Government policies that seek to increase economic growth through both direct and indirect manipulation of the channels affecting technological change are then considered. A key finding of the book, as contained in chapter two, is that in some cases, government efforts to increase economic growth may actually have the opposite effect in the short-term before eventually yielding the desired results.

The first chapter identifies competition in research and development and in output markets as key determinants of the intensity of research and development (R&D) efforts. These efforts are then shown to determine the pace of technological change and of industrial evolution. The extent of competition in an industry is endogenously derived and relationships between this variable and research efforts, equilibrium prices and quantities, profitability, and input demands by firms are derived. A preliminary empirical examination of some of these relationships is also undertaken.

The second chapter develops a general equilibrium model of an economy with imperfect competition to study the relative roles played in the process of economic growth by investments in physical capital and in R&D. Even when competitive forces prevent the implementation of the results of most of the research that takes place, it is shown that the long-run rate of economic growth is positively dependent on both the extent of competition and firm research intensities. These variables, and therefore the rate of economic growth, are demonstrated to be affected by fiscal policy. A reduction of government, with lower wage taxes, is shown to increase competition and research intensities leading to a higher growth rate in the steady state. However, the immediate impact of such a policy is demonstrated to be in the opposite direction, with a prolonged period of lower growth rates of output and capital during a transition phase.

The third chapter examines the externality generated by newly created goods on research efforts. This positive externality, in the form of a knowledge spillover, is shown to be vital to obtain sustained growth. It is argued that with large private costs to adopt and adapt existing knowledge for use in research, diffusion of enough new knowledge necessary to increase research productivity is unlikely to occur and, therefore, economic growth could eventually cease. Government, through a tax-subsidy system aimed at disseminating newly created knowledge can, however, revive economic growth. The optimal level of such a tax scheme, in terms of maximizing the rate of economic growth, is derived and characterized. This chapter also discusses the relationship between monopoly power and economic growth. The positive impact on economic growth, through the destruction of monopoly power, of governmental dissemination of knowledge is studied.

Acknowledgments

This book had its origins as a Ph.D. dissertation in Economics at the University of Pennsylvania. I am deeply grateful to my primary advisor, Fumio Hayashi, for his advice and encouragement. Fumio was extremely supportive in countless ways throughout my graduate student days. Among other things, he read many early drafts of this work and made innumerable suggestions that have improved its quality. I am also indebted to Raphael Rob, Boyan Jovanovic, Costas Azariadis and Lee Ohanian, all of whom were my teachers at Penn. I have learned much of the economics of technological innovations from my many conversations with Rafi and Boyan. I would like to thank Costas for encouraging me to work in growth theory and to Lee for so graciously stepping in as an advisor. I am also deeply indebted to one of my first teachers of economics, Robert Gitter, for stimulating my interest in the discipline and in encouraging me to pursue a career as an economist.

Writing a dissertation is often a lonely period fraught with frustrations. My many friends and colleagues at Penn deserve a great deal of gratitude for making my experience more enjoyable. In particular, I am grateful for the intellectual companionship and friendships of: Jean-Marc Tallon, Pedro Ferreira, Kamal Saggi, Adel Varghese, Per Fredrickson, Doug Schuman, Claudia Stachel, Anne Kertula, Juuso Valimaki, Nikos Vettas and Mary Thomson. I am especially indebted to Rohit Verma, an old friend as well as a colleague at Penn. Rohit has always been a great friend and at Penn was also a fun roommate and an always willing discussant of my work, providing valuable insights towards solutions.

As in all my endeavors, my parents Sachit and Manju Panth, were very supportive during the process of writing this book. I am grateful to my father for having implanted and nourished the intellectual curiosity that led to this effort and to my mother for her moral support. As always, I am deeply indebted to my wife Karen who has made my frustrations tolerable and all my successes and accomplishments more joyful.

Technological Innovation, Industrial Evolution, and Economic Growth

I

Competition, Innovation, and Productivity Growth

Output market competition and rivalry in research and development are closely related and one influences the other. The technology of production, acquired through research and development (R&D), is an important determinant of market competition and of prices charged and quantities produced. Competition in output markets, however, leads to the search for new and improved technologies. In a Schumpeterian world, it is the monopoly profits garnered in output markets that serve as incentives for firms to undertake costly research and development. Technological progress, the fruit of these efforts at innovation, however, determines the evolution of market structure through time and of the continuous process of creation and destruction of monopoly power.

To examine these relationships, this chapter constructs a model of an industry with a number of products and firms competing to improve the technologies of production. It is shown that the intensity of competition in research and the expected profits resulting from output market competition determine the magnitude of research conducted by an individual firm. This, in turn, stochastically determines the technologies that it discovers. These firms face nontrivial decisions regarding the development of their newly-discovered technologies. Those that do proceed with development compete in the output market and garner the profits in whose expectation they competed in research; those that do not develop their technologies earn no profits. Over time, these repeated innovations result in the evolution of technologies across products in the industry and the concurrent evolution of prices charged and quantities produced. The model developed in this chapter, therefore, provides insights concerning the evolution of an industry through a Schumpeterian process.

The underlying structure of the model is straightforward. Time is discrete and new vintages of technology arrive each period as long as research expenditure is positive. Firms compete in determining the extent of each innovation, i.e. in determining the contribution of each vintage of technology in improving their factor productivities. These improvements determine the number of firms that successfully produce in the output markets and the size of their profits and input demands upon production.

Empirical implications concerning competition in research, and competition in the output market are derived from the model as are relationships between the intensities of such competition and observable profits and input demands. The empirical evidence regarding these implications are also briefly examined in this chapter.

Although many aspects of the economics of technological improvement have been previously studied by industrial organization economists, the model constructed in this chapter lends some novel insights. Papers by Loury (1979), Lee & Wilde (1980) and Reinganum (1982) are prominent examples of earlier work done in this area. In a timing of innovation paradigm, where firms compete in being the first to discover an innovation of a given size, the papers cited above study the incentives for undertaking costly technological innovations and examine how such efforts are affected by competition in R&D. While they shed considerable light on how competition in research affects research intensities, the relationship between R&D and output market competition cannot be examined in the models developed in these papers as they abstract away from this issue. In addition, only a single innovation is considered and the size of that innovation--in terms of its contribution to improving quality or reducing costs is fixed exogenously. Empirical implications concerning the extent of improvements in factor productivities at points in time, therefore, cannot be derived from these models.

Although Lach and Rob (1992) provide a theory of repeated technological innovation in an industry and also explicitly consider competition in the output market, there are significant differences between their model and the one constructed here. Lach and Rob do derive empirical implications concerning the casualty between research and development and investment in physical capital. However, the size of each innovation is given in their model and the question of relevance is when it is discovered, not how large it is. Thus the relationship between competition in the output market and the size of innovations cannot be examined in the context of their paper.

In this chapter a relationship between competition in R&D and competition in output markets is derived by explicitly incorporating competition in output markets into the model. Since we are able to observe concentration in output markets, we are thus able to derive empirically verifiable relationships between research inputs and the intensity of competition in various industries. The model in this chapter also derives a measure of total factor productivity growth at the industrial level and shows that it depends on the intensity of competition.

The model of industrial evolution through endogenous technological change considered in this chapter is put to additional uses in the following chapter. It is integrated into a general equilibrium framework there and contributes to our understanding of macroeconomic issues. Additionally, an implication of a finding made there is that the R&D process examined by us here implies that the log of total factor productivity at the product level is a random walk. Predicting future technological innovations for a particular good through an analysis of the past is, therefore, unlikely to prove very fruitful.

The remainder of this chapter is organized below as follows: Section 2 explicitly defines what we mean by an industry and examines the competition in output markets at a point in time. In this section, the results of the research and development process are taken as given. Section 3 builds upon the previous section to determine the equilibrium research and development process. Section 4 discusses the empirical implications of the equilibrium found in the preceding section and section 5 briefly examines some of these implications. The final section contains concluding remarks.

1.2 PRODUCTION AND OUTPUT MARKET COMPETITION

This section describes what we mean by an industry, the nature of competition in the output markets of the industry and the production functions for the various product lines in the industry. Competition in, and the outcome of, the research and development process are described in the following section and for the time being we shall take that as given.

An industry is composed of a continuum of goods or product lines whose measure has been normalized to be one. We shall index a product line within the industry by $i \in [0,1]$. The industry has a finite number of producing firms in period t: n_{t-1} drawn from some underlying universe of potential firms: N. The subscript of n is denoted by t-1 rather than t because this number is determined in the preceding period through the R&D process. We treat N as an exogenous parameter of the industry given by historical and institutional factors. For the moment we shall take n_{t-1} as simply given; the next section elaborates on how the selection of n_{t-1} from N is determined.

Product lines within an industry have different production technologies. However, within any industry the technologies of production share enough common attributes that firms possessing experience with the technology of any product line within the industry can compete effectively in the generation of newer vintages of technologies for the production of other product lines in the same industry. Therefore, in each period all N firms can compete in production and research. However, as will be shown in the next section, the equilibrium of the R&D process dictates that only a subset, n_{t-1}, of the N firms will actually produce anything.

In essence, product lines are grouped into industries on the basis of some underlying feature of their production technologies rather than strictly on the basis of any degree of substitutability or some explicit physical properties of the product lines. By an industry, we have in mind then a group of products whose technologies of production are similar enough that entry barriers into either research

or production do not exist for any producers in the same industry whereas such barriers are prohibitive for firms outside the industry.
The demand function for product line i is given by:

$$Q_t(i) = \frac{I_t}{P_t(i)}$$

where $P_t(i)$ is the price of the product. I_t is a parameter of the demand function that firms in the industry take as given. For the purpose of this chapter, it can be interpreted as the size of the demand function. Such demand functions can be derived from either utility maximization problems or from cost minimization problems. For example suppose each agent in the economy has an income level w_t and the following utility function:

$$u\left(\int_o^J \int_0^I \ln Q_t(i,j) didj\right)$$

where j is an index of industries and i is an index of product lines within a given industry j'. Then

$$I_t = \frac{mw_t}{IJ}$$

where m is the measure of agents in the economy.

Alternatively, suppose industries produce intermediate goods used in the production of a final good y_t in the following fashion:

$$y_t = \exp\left[\int_0^1 \int_0^1 \ln Q_t(i,j) didj\right]$$

where again j denotes industries and i denotes product lines within industries. Then $I_t = y_t$ has the interpretation of being gross domestic product. Either interpretation is valid for the purposes of this chapter, except for some of the empirical examinations in section 6 where the latter interpretation is used.

Technologies of production are governed by a patent system. Once a patent expires any firm in the industry can use the patented technology. The length of the patent protection period is assumed to be one and therefore the state-of-the-art technologies of vintage t-1 for the production of each product line within the industry is common knowledge for all the firms in the industry in period t. We denote these technologies by $A_{t-1}^*(i)$, and they have the interpretation of being total factor productivity available to these firms at the product-line level.

The current "best" technology for the product line is, however, denoted by $A_t^*(i)$, and only one firm possesses that technology. The equilibrium outcome of the R&D process described in the following section ensures that each of the n_{t-1} firms exclusively possesses rights to such technologies, technologies of vintage t, for the production of exactly $\left(\frac{1}{n_{t-1}}\right)$ th of the measure of product lines in the industry. Therefore for each product line, while all firms possess $A_{t-1}^*(i)$, only one firm has access to technology of vintage t.

As illustrated in detail later on, all firms do engage in R&D in order to improve the technology of each and every product line within the industry in period t-1. However, the equilibrium will dictate that only the discoverer of the "best" technology for any product will actually develop it for use in production. For the purposes of this section, we shall take the distribution of technologies across firms as described above and focus on the nature of the resulting output market competition.

In period t, each intermediate good can be produced using technologies of vintage t and earlier in the following fashion:

$$Q_t(i) = A_\tau^*(i) k_t^\alpha(i) l_t^{1-\alpha}(i) \qquad\qquad \tau = 0, ..., t$$

where $k_t(i)$ and $l_t(i)$ are capital and labor inputs into production.

As the production function is linearly homogeneous in its arguments, associated with the use of each vintage of technology is a unit cost function:

$$\frac{C_{(w_t, R_t)}}{A_\tau^*(i)}$$

where w_t and R_t are the cost of labor and the user cost of capital, respectively.

With regard to the form of competition in the output market, we postulate Bertrand competition. With such competition, for each product line the possessor of the most efficient technology supplies the entire amount demanded at the price that is equal to the unit cost of production of the next-most efficient producer. Given the unit elasticity of the conditional demand function for each intermediate good $Q_t(i)$, this will be true regardless of the difference in unit costs between different firms. In effect, the most efficient producer is always constrained above in her choice of price by the cost of her competitors and, therefore, regardless of the difference in unit costs, cannot completely disregard this and act as a monopolist in setting prices. In the jargon of the innovation literature, unit elasticity of the demand function enables us to abstract away from the issue of drastic versus non drastic innovations. In that literature, a drastic innovation is considered to be one where the innovation confers on the innovator such an advantage over competitors (in terms of quality, cost or some other dimension) that she can effectively ignore the competition and behave as a monopolist in the output market. The incentives regarding R&D differ between current incumbents and potential entrants depending on whether the innovation sought is drastic or not in the exponential date-of-discovery paradigm of patent races. For more on this see Tirole (1988). We avoid this complication with our assumptions of Bertrand competition and a patent period of one in addition to the unit elasticity of the demand function.

In our model, as technologies of later vintages are at least as efficient as those of earlier vintages, the sole possessor of vintage t technology for product i will capture the entire market and price at the unit cost corresponding to technology of vintage t-1, the most efficient vintage available to its competitors. If innovations in technology are multiplicative, i.e. $A^*_\tau(i) = \gamma^*_\tau(i) A^*_{\tau-1}(i)$, $\gamma^*_\tau(\cdot) \in \left[1, \bar{\gamma}\right]$; the resulting price and quantity supplied are:

$$P_t(i) = \frac{C_{(w_t, R_t)}}{A^*_{t-1}(i)} \quad \text{and} \quad Q_t(i) = \frac{A^*_{t-1}(i) \cdot I_t}{C_{(w_t, R_t)}} ;$$

and the input demands of the producing firm are:

$$k_{t}(i) = \frac{\alpha \cdot I_{t}}{\gamma_{t}^{*}(i) \cdot R_{t}}, \qquad \text{and} \qquad l_{t}(i) = \frac{(1-\alpha) \cdot I_{t}}{\gamma_{t}^{*}(i) \cdot w_{t}}. \tag{1.1}$$

The producing firm's profit in product i is a fraction of total sales, whose magnitude depends on the technological innovation, $\gamma_{t}^{*}(\cdot)$:

$$\left[1 - \frac{1}{\gamma_{t}^{*}(i)}\right] \cdot I_{t} \quad = \quad \left[1 - \frac{1}{\gamma_{t}^{*}(i)}\right] \cdot P_{t}(i) Q_{t}(i) \tag{1.2}$$

1.3 RESEARCH AND DEVELOPMENT

1.3.1 Description of the Research Process

We shall assume that conventions governing intellectual property are such that exclusive usage of a newly discovered technology by the discoverer is feasible for only one period. In practice, this would correspond to the extension of patent protection for a period of one. At the end of the period the innovation becomes common property that can be used by anyone. However, this period of patent protection applies only to the usage of the technology in production and not to the use of the newly discovered technology in scientific efforts at further innovations. Again in practice this would arise from the fact that the filers of patent protection claims are required to submit the technological specifications of their discoveries to the patent authority where it is available for perusal by the general public. The effect of such patent structures, seen for example in the United States, would be that although the discoverer of a new technology is protected by law for a finite period of time from having competitors use her innovation in production, she is on an equal footing with regard to her competitors in building upon her innovations to generate the next vintage of technology.

During period t-1 these patent-holders compete with the N-1 other potential producing firms in the industry in generating the next vintage of technology to be used in production during the following period. This competition in research will be the focus of this section.

Note that at the same time, the patent-holders are also competing in the output market with other firms, who are legally allowed to use only technologies of earlier vintages for production purposes, in the manner outlined in the previous section.

The R&D process for any industry is a three-step process where all N firms first decide whether to pay a fixed cost to engage in R&D at all or not. Following this, those that do decide to engage in R&D simultaneously decide their research intensities that stochastically determine the technology parameters that they discover for the product lines aimed at by their research. Finally, the firms have to decide whether to develop their technologies for use or not.

There is usually a fixed cost associated with engaging in research and development that involves the purchase of research equipment and the hiring of at least some research support personnel. The first step of the R&D decision process is meant to capture this by requiring the hiring of a fixed amount of labor if any research is to be engaged in at all. We assume that once this fixed cost is paid, firms can target their variable research efforts at as many or as few of the product lines within the industry as they choose. The outcome of the research process for each product line is specific to the amount of variable research effort targeted at that particular product line; i.e. whereas the fixed cost of entry is independent of the number of product lines research is to be conducted in, variable research intensities are product-line specific. In the absence of any inter-product-line research externalities, firms that pay the fixed cost would engage in separate research efforts at discovering better technologies for each and every product line within the industry as long as expected profit from conducting research in that line is non negative.

Once the outcome of the research efforts is known, firms need to decide whether to develop this discovery into a form that can be used in production or not. In practice, development consists of modifying the technology to work effectively with labor. For example it could involve making the new technology "user friendly" or retraining workers to work with the new machinery embodying the new technology. For analytical simplicity, we assume that although firms do need to decide whether to develop a new technology or not, actual development costs are zero.

Since we will be focusing on the R&D process in period t-1, we will drop the time subscripts of variables denoting research costs. We shall denote the fixed labor requirement for each firm engaging in research in the industry by $\bar{x}$, and the variable research intensity, measured in units of labor, targeted by firm s at product line i by $x^s(i)$. The decision process of the firms can be summarized by the following diagram:

Figure I
Research and Development Decision Tree

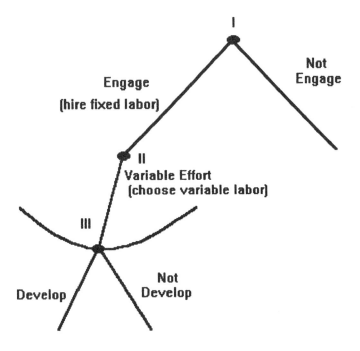

The equilibrium concept that we focus on for the research game is a symmetric subgame perfect Nash equilibrium. In equilibrium, as we will see below, the decision processes of the firms in different periods will turn out to be fully separable. Therefore, fully rational firms will need to only consider the outcomes in the product markets in the following period when making their research decisions in period t-1. We will, for the time being, confine ourselves to the case where firms indeed consider only the following period and then show that this is fully rational.

A note on terminology--we shall refer to profits gained in the production sector as *operating profits*. Operating profits are profits before adjusting for research costs in stage II. After operating profits have been discounted and research costs encountered in stage II deducted, we shall refer to the quantity as *profits from research*. Profits from research then take into account variable research costs but not the fixed cost of engaging. Once this has been adjusted for, i.e. the costs of engaging has been subtracted from profits from research in all product lines in which research is conducted, we shall refer to the magnitude as *profit from engaging*.

1.3.2 Equilibrium in the Period R&D Game

The equilibrium of stage III of the game will have only the discoverer of the most efficient technology, or the *winner*, developing it for use in production. Consider the decision faced by the other firms. If the winner develops his technology, they are indifferent between developing their technologies or not. If they do develop them, the winner will outprice them and they will make zero operating profits in the ensuing Bertrand equilibrium in the period t product market. If, on the other hand, they do not develop their technologies, then the most efficient technology with which they can produce in period t will be the technology of vintage t-1, $A_{t-1}^*(i)$, whose patent protection will have expired and will, therefore, be accessible to all firms. As the technology of the winner in period t will be at least as efficient as this vintage, all but the winner will still make zero profits.

We assume that those who are not winners choose not to develop their technologies given that regardless of their development decision, they will not make any profits in the period t output market, In the presence of even an infinitesimal cost of development, they would indeed strictly prefer this strategy. The best response by the discoverer of the best technology is then to develop her technology and compete in the following period's output market against all other firms. In the period t market for product i, we then observe a two-point distribution of technologies across firms, with a single firm possessing vintage t technology, $A_{t(i)}^*$ and all others having access to vintage t-1 technology, $A_{t-1(i)}^*$.

The winning firm's profit in period t will depend upon its technological lead over the previous period's vintage. At stage II, suppose n of the N potential firms engage in research aimed at improving the technology of product line i. At the end of stage II, let firm s have improved upon the vintage t-1 technology by a multiplicative factor $\gamma_{t(i)}^s$, s = 1, ..., n ; $\gamma_{t(i)}^s \varepsilon [1,\bar{\gamma}]$. Then from the outcome of the development decision and the resultant output market competition in the following period; by (1.2) we have period t operating profit of firm s in product i:

$$\left[1 - \frac{1}{\gamma_t^s(i)}\right] \cdot I_t \quad \text{if } \gamma_t^s(i) > \gamma_t^{s'}(i); \quad \forall s \neq s' \tag{1.3}$$

$$0 \qquad \text{otherwise.}$$

The profit of the winner depends stochastically on its research intensity. Each firm's technological innovation, $\gamma_{t(i)}^s$, is determined by the intensity of its research in stage II of the game when each participating firm simultaneously chooses the amount of labor: $x^s(i)$, that it is devoting to improving the technology of product i. This choice of labor stochastically determines the magnitude of the innovation in technology, $\gamma_{t(i)}^s$ and, therefore, the size of potential profits for the winner. In other words $\gamma_{t(i)}^s$ is a random draw from a conditional cumulative distribution function $F(\gamma, x^s(i))$ with support $[1,\bar{\gamma}]$, such that:

$$\frac{\partial}{\partial x} F(\gamma, x) > 0;$$

$$\lim_{x \to 0} F(\gamma, x) = 1 \quad \forall \gamma > 1$$

$$\lim_{x \to \infty} F(\gamma, x) = 0 \quad \forall \gamma \leq \bar{\gamma}.$$

The first-order stochastic dominance requirements we assume above state that a firm's innovation to technology, which is multiplicative, is: a) at least one (no loss of knowledge), b) exactly one if no research effort is targeted at improving the technology (no costless exogenous technological improvement), and, c) increases in expected value with more research expenditure.

We specialize the functional form of the R&D technology in order to analyze the nature of the symmetric equilibrium resulting in the subgame starting at stage II. Accordingly, we assume that

$$F(\gamma, x^s{}_{(i)}) = \left[\frac{\bar{\gamma}(\gamma-1)}{\gamma(\bar{\gamma}-1)}\right]^{\lambda x^s{}_{(i)}}, \qquad \lambda > 0.$$

Note that this cumulative distribution function satisfies our requirements concerning the stochastic dominance requirements. λ is to be interpreted as the productivity of labor in research. The larger λ is, the larger the expected value of the innovation to total factor productivity for any given level of research intensity.

At the beginning of stage II, all n firms participating in research aimed at improving the technology of product line i, simultaneously choose variable research intensities to maximize the expectation of their period t operating profits in market i as given by (1.3). In calculating expected operating profits, firms take into account the statement in (1.3) that positive profits can be expected only if they are the winner, i.e. the one who discovers the largest innovation in TFP over the technology of current vintage. In the appendix it is shown that a firm choosing research intensity $x^s{}_{(i)}$ calculates its expected period t operating profits in market i to be:

$$\left[1-\frac{1}{\tau}\right]\frac{\lambda x^s{}_{(i)}}{\lambda x^s{}_{(i)} + \lambda a_{(i)} + 1}\cdot I_t; \qquad a_{(i)} = \sum_{s'\neq s} x^{s'}{}_{(i)}.$$

$x^s{}_{(i)}$, the research intensity that firm s targets at product line i, is measured in units of labor. $a_{(i)}$ is therefore total research labor targeted at improving the technology of product line i by all of the competitors of firm s. The larger the research intensity of firm s, the larger its expected innovation to TFP and therefore the larger the profits. The appearance of $a_{(i)}$ in the denominator reflects the fact that regardless of how large the innovation of s is, its profits will be zero if some other firm discovers a larger innovation. Thus the more its competitors increase their research intensities, the less chance firm s has of being the "winner" and therefore the lower its expected profits.

Firm s chooses variable research intensity for product i, $x^s{}_{(i)}$, to maximize its expected profit from research in that product line net of variable research costs:

$$\max_{x^s{}_{(i)}} \left[1-\tfrac{1}{\gamma}\right] \frac{\lambda x^s{}_{(i)}}{\lambda x^s{}_{(i)} + \lambda a_{(i)} + 1} \cdot \frac{I_t}{R_t} - w_{t-1} x^s{}_{(i)}, \qquad (1.4)$$

The first-order condition for this problem is:

$$\left[1-\tfrac{1}{\gamma}\right] \frac{\lambda(\lambda a_{(i)} + 1)}{(\lambda x^s{}_{(i)} + \lambda a_{(i)} + 1)^2} \cdot \frac{I_t}{R_t w_{t-1}} - 1 = 0;$$

which is analogous to the one faced by firms in Loury's timing of innovation paradigm, where firms race over time to be the first to arrive at an innovation with an exogenously given value. If labor productivity in research (λ) is large enough so as to at least enable a firm to profitably conduct research in the absence of any competition (i.e. an interior solution to the monopolist's problem exists--a reasonable enough assumption), we have:

Proposition I: A symmetric Nash equilibrium exists where each firm invests a strictly positive amount in research targeted at product line i. Furthermore, the amount of labor hired by a firm to engage in research in product line i depends only on the number of its competitors n-1 ,and on the ratio of the present value of sales in period t in that product line to unit research costs :

$$\left(\frac{P_t(i) \cdot Q_t(i)}{R_t w_{t-1}}\right).$$

Proof: Existence of an interior equilibrium follows Loury (1979). The fact that variable research effort depends on

$$\frac{I_t}{R_t w_{t-1}} = \frac{P_t(i) Q_t(i)}{R_t w_{t-1}}$$

is evident from the first order condition.

In the symmetric Nash equilibrium for the subgame starting at stage II, we see that each of the n firms invests an equal amount of labor in improving the technology of product line i and that amount depends on both its chances of being the winner and the size of its profit if it is indeed the winner. The number of competitors is a crucial variable affecting the decision as it determines the chances of being the innovator with the largest innovation. The expected total sales per unit research costs is an additional important determinant since by (1.2), period t operating profits of the producing firm in market i is a fraction of total sales. The higher sales per unit research costs, the larger operating profits would be upon winning the innovation game, and therefore the more the incentive to increase research intensity would be.

As the above discussion would imply, and the next proposition proves, in equilibrium each firm's research input into a particular product line decreases with the number of its competitors engaged in research in that product.

We also find that each of the firms that does participate in any kind of research will, in equilibrium, invest equal amounts of labor targeted at improving each product line in the industry. This arises from the fact that while $\Pi_t^*(i)$, the Nash solution to (1.4), is found to be decreasing in competition, it is strictly positive whenever only a finite number of firms is conducting research. Therefore, once a firm has paid the fixed cost of research in stage I, its expected profit from research in each product line is strictly positive and so it may as well conduct separate research efforts at improving each and every product line in the industry. Since product lines and research strategies are symmetric within industries, each one of the firm's competitors will also follow the same strategy. Due to all this symmetry, in the subgame starting at stage II, each firm that has paid the fixed costs of research will thus act in an identical manner with regard to each product line.

The discussion above is summarized in the following proposition, whose proof is in the appendix.

Proposition II: If n_j firms pay the fixed cost of doing research in the industry, each of the firms will invest

$$x^*(n_j - 1, v_t) > 0; \text{ where } v_t = \frac{P_t(i)Q_t(i)}{R_t w_{t-1}} = \frac{I_t}{R_t w_{t-1}};$$

in variable research labor in *each* product line i in the industry. Expected profit from research in each product line is given by:

$$\Pi_t^*(n_j - 1, v_t) > 0 ,$$

the Nash solution to (1.4). Expected profit from research and research efforts are strictly decreasing in n_j and strictly increasing in v_t.

Now consider the first stage of the R&D game where the N firms in the industry decide whether to pay the fixed cost of research or not. We will see that in the Nash equilibrium at that stage, each of the N firms will choose to engage in research with the same probability q_{t-1}.

Consider the problem from the perspective of a particular firm s. If it along with exactly n-1 of its competitors does pay the fixed cost, then it will compete in research in each of the product lines $i \in [0,1]$, in the manner outlined above. By investing $x^*(\cdot)$ in a particular product line, firm s, therefore, expects a profit from research of $\Pi_t^*(n_j - 1, v_t)$ in that product line. Since the measure of products in the industry is 1 and expected profit from research is the same in each product, total *industry-wide* expected profit from engagement for firm s is:

$$\Pi_t^*(n_j - 1, v_t) - w_{t-1}\bar{x};\qquad(1.5)$$

where $\bar{x}$ is the units of labor, interpreted as research support personnel, that a firm interested in conducting research in the industry has to hire before any research can be undertaken. Since $\Pi_t^*(n_j - 1, v_t)$ is decreasing in n, so is (1.5). We further assume that $w_{t-1}\bar{x}$ is not so large that a firm facing no competition in research would not pay the fixed cost. We also assume that if n = N, i.e. all the potential firms do enter the research game, (1.5) is negative (a large enough N and a large enough support-personnel requirement will ensure that this condition is met). Given, then, that at least one firm will always find it profitable to pay the fixed cost and set up research whereas if all firms do so, each one of them will make a loss; there will exist a probability $q_{t-1} \in (0,1)$ such that if each of the other N-1 firms engages in research with that probability, the Nth firm will also be indifferent between engaging in research or not. This probability reflects the profitability of conducting research and therefore depends on v_t as well as on N and $\bar{x}$.

We therefore find that the expected profit from a particular product line prior to entry is in equilibrium equal to zero. Given that each firm is indifferent between entering in research or not, firm s evaluates the number of competitors it will face in stage II if it itself engages in research, as being a random number n-1, drawn from a binomial distribution with parameters N-1 and q_{t-1}. Upon the realization of n-1, if firm s has also paid the fixed cost, it will compete with all of the n-1 of its competitors in research in *each* of the product lines of the entire industry (containing a unit measure of product lines) in a symmetric fashion. Expected *industry-wide* profit from engagement for each firm is then a binomial expectation of (1.5) with respect to n-1 and is also identically equal to zero:

$$\hat{\Pi}(q_{t-1}, N_j, v_t) \equiv 0.\qquad(1.6)$$

The expected profit from engagement, $\hat{\Pi}(q_{t-1}, N, v_t)$, is as to be expected from our analyses of the underlying functions in the previous two propositions, increasing in v_t, the ratio of sales to unit research costs, and decreasing with more competition in research, q_{t-1}. The latter term is a measure of the intensity of competition in R&D as for any given N , the higher the probability with which any firm enters the research game, the more intense competition is likely to be in stage II of the research process when firms are choosing their research intensities.

1.3.3 Dynamic R&D Equilibrium

The firm's infinite horizon problem collapses to a series of one period problems analyzed above. In each period t, it will be faced with the same three-stage decision process concerning research. If in each period in the future, the firm and all of its competitors play according to the one period equilibrium strategies examined earlier, by (1.6) expected profits from engagement in each period in the future will be zero. The firm then does not have to consider the repercussions of its present research decisions on the future beyond operating profits one period hence. Thus, given the strategies of its competitors, the strategy considered so far is indeed optimal for each firm in the infinite horizon game as well.

In the language of game theory, the assumptions that patents expire after one period and that there are enough firms such that profits are negative if all of them engage in research in equilibrium, guarantees that with our equilibrium strategies, the state variable in each industry--the distribution of the current vintage of technologies across product lines, $A_t^*(i)$, does not affect the nature of the current problem faced by the firms. The game then becomes fully separable and we can essentially consider the research game in each period as being a stage game in the infinite horizon game with no real state variable. The equilibrium strategies considered above then constitute Markov Nash equilibrium strategies in the infinite horizon game. The above argument is summarized in the following proposition, whose formal proof is in the appendix:

Proposition III:

$$\left\langle \sigma_\tau^* \right\rangle_{\tau=0}^\infty = \left\langle q_\tau, \left(x^*_{(n-1,\nu_{t+1})}\right), \left(\text{develop iff} \gamma_\tau^s{}_{(i)} > \gamma_\tau^{s'}{}_{(i)}\right)\right\rangle$$

constitutes a symmetric Markov Nash equilibrium strategy for each firm in each industry in the infinite-horizon research game, given the equilibrium Bertrand outcome in the product market for each good. The first element of $\sigma_\tau^*(\cdot)$ is the decision regarding engaging in research in period t, the second the variable research effort and the third the decision regarding development.

1.4 IMPLICATIONS FOR INDUSTRIAL STRUCTURE

The model of R&D and production constructed in the previous sections has implications concerning a number of observable variables. As we will see, the set of producing firms in the industry in period t coincides perfectly with the set of firms that participated in research in that industry in the previous period. Implications of this variable on total factor productivity growth at the industrial level are elaborated upon below. Implications concerning firm and industrial profitability, input demands and intensities of research are also discussed.

The symmetry in the model, in combination with the continuum assumption regarding the number of products in the industry, ensures that producing firms in a given period are exactly those that conducted research the previous period. Since only firms that participate in research in period t-1 improve upon existing factor productivities, the set of firms actually producing in period t is drawn from this set. Furthermore, since each of the firms participating in research conducts research in the technology of each good in the industry and there is a continuum of goods within each industry, each of the n_{t-1} firms "wins" the research game for at least one product. Therefore each firm that paid the fixed cost of research in the previous period will produce at least one product during the present. The set of producing firms in the industry in period t therefore coincides perfectly with the set of firms that participated in research in that industry in the previous period and we shall continue to use the notation n_{t-1} for this set of firms.

A note regarding the nature of the variables whose relationships we are discussing and the implications concerning the effect of exogenous variables is required at this point. All the implications of the model discussed below involve the relationships between the number of firms producing and variables such as research intensities, profits and input demands. However, the number of firms producing in the industry is itself an endogenous variable in our model and hence the relationships discussed are those between two endogenous variables. If all industries are identical regarding the fixed cost of entry into research, research labor productivity and the measure of product lines, then the observed characteristics of the industries, namely number of firms, profits et cetera would be identical across industries except for some error term. Variations in the number of firms and the other endogenous variables being considered would not be observed.

However, all industries are not identical. They differ in their fixed costs, their productivity in research and in the number of product lines that they have. A proper empirical test of the model would involve testing the variation of the endogenous variables, including number of firms, as a function of the variation in the exogenous variables such as the fixed cost of research. These latter variables however are unfortunately often not observable or are unavailable.

We are thus left with observable relationships between endogenous variables such as research intensities, profits and input demands on the one hand and the number of producing firms, itself an endogenous variable on the other hand. Any variation in an exogenous variable, such as research productivity, would affect the number of firms and, through this *as well as possibly directly,* the other endogenous variables being considered.

For example consider the productivity of workers in research. A change in this variable would simultaneously affect the number of firms and research inputs and therefore the relationship between these two variables would vary across industries depending on their research productivities. However, if the fixed costs of research increased it would directly affect only the number of firms in research (which would decrease) and would affect other endogenous variables such as research inputs only indirectly through changes in the number of firms.

In what follows we are therefore assuming that exogenous variables that affect both the number of firms as well as other endogenous variables directly are constant across industries. However, variables that directly affect only the number of firms and affect other variables only indirectly through changes in the number of firms are allowed to vary across industries. If exogenous variables that directly affect the *relationship* between the observed endogenous variables vary across industries then the implications considered below would not hold. Given this caveat, we now proceed to these implications.

First consider implications of the model concerning firm-level and industry-wide research intensities. As discussed in proposition II, variable labor input into research per firm per product line, $x_{t-1}^*(\cdot)$, is decreasing in the number of firms engaged in research and increasing in the ratio of total sales to unit research costs. As firms face more competition, their chances of being the one to discover the largest innovation decreases and therefore so does their incentive to spend in research. However, conditional on being the one with the largest innovation, the expected value of that innovation and therefore of operating profits, increases with research input. This latter effect provides an incentive to increase research efforts. The net effects of these two incentives is, as proved below, that whereas firms decrease their research input with competition, they do not decrease it by enough to reduce total input, i.e. the research inputs of all the firms put together, $n_{t-1}x^*(\cdot)$, increases. This is true in Loury's model as well, although there the incentive to increase research input is provided by the decrease in the expected time lag before the arrival of the innovation rather than its expected magnitude which is exogenously given.

Second, consider the implications of the model concerning profits and improvements in total factor productivities. Increased competition and therefore lower research input per firm, leads the Nash solution to (1.4) excluding research costs, i.e. the discounted expected period t operating profits in good i for a particular firm:

$$\left[1-\tfrac{1}{\gamma}\right]\frac{\lambda x^*(\cdot)}{\lambda n_{t-1}x^*(\cdot)+1}\cdot\frac{I_t}{R_t}$$

to decline with n_{t-1} as is verified from the proof of proposition II (see appendix). This is because the above is calculated by taking into account the fact that operating profits will be non zero only if the innovation discovered by the calculating firm is indeed the largest one. Note that this expected profit is the discounted expectation of: (1.3):

$$\left[1 - \frac{1}{\gamma_t^s(i)}\right] \cdot I_t \quad \text{iff} \gamma_t^s(i) > \gamma_t^{s'}(i); \quad \forall s \neq s';$$

$$0 \qquad \qquad \text{otherwise.}$$

The *actual* period t operating profit in product i is however:

$$\left[1 - \frac{1}{\gamma_t^*(i)}\right] \cdot I_t; \; \gamma_t^*(i) = \max_s\left[\gamma_t^s(i)\right], \quad s = 1, \ldots, n_{t-1} \qquad (1.7)$$

where $\gamma_t^*(i)$ is the implemented innovation in total factor productivity in period t, $A_t^*(i) = \gamma_t^*(i)A_{t-1}^*(i)$. If n_{t-1} firms participate in research in period t-1, the innovation in TFP, $\gamma_t^*(i)$ is a random variable drawn from $[1, \bar{\gamma}]$, with a conditional cumulative distribution function:

$$F(\gamma, n_{t-1}x^s(i)) = \left[\frac{\bar{\gamma}(\gamma - 1)}{\gamma(\bar{\gamma} - 1)}\right]^{\lambda n_{t-1}x^s(i)}, \qquad \lambda > 0.$$

The distribution of $\gamma_t^*(i)$, however, depends on total research intensity: $n_{t-1}x^*(i)$ and not solely on the research of a single firm. Since total research, $n_{t-1}x^*(i)$, is increasing in the number of participating firms so is the expectation of $\gamma_t^*(i)$ by the first-order stochastic dominance properties of the CDF: $F(\cdot)$. As a result, the expectation of (1.7) is also *increasing* in competition. This is because, unlike in the expectation of (1.3), the identity of the innovating firm is irrelevant. Therefore, although expected operating profits for any particular firm prior to the realization of the technological discoveries is decreasing in competition, by the above discussion the expected operating profit of the *winner*, i.e. the producer in period t, is increasing in n_{t-1}. We thus expect the implemented innovation in TFP and the operating profit of the producing firm in a product line to be positively correlated with the number of firms that engaged in research in the previous period and therefore are producing (albeit in different product lines) in the industry at present.

Realized *industry-wide* operating profits are also increasing in competition. Each of the n_{t-1} firms that pay the fixed cost of research in period t-1 conducts research in each of the product lines i in the industry in a symmetric fashion. Furthermore, product lines are symmetric within industries. Therefore realized operating profit in period t in each product line is a random variable given by (1.7). Given the symmetry of strategies and product lines and the actual number of firms that engage in research in the industry, n_{t-1}, these random variables are identically and independently drawn across product lines in the industry. Since the measure of product lines within the industry is unity, conditional on n_{t-1}, realized industry-wide operating profits are by the law of large numbers, exactly equal to the expectation of (1.7) and are therefore also increasing in competition. Let $\overline{\Pi}_t\left(n_{t-1}, v_t, I_t\right)$ denote this quantity. Note, however, that this use of the law of large numbers is not without its technical problems. Nevertheless, for the mathematical constructs that enable us to do this see Judd (1985) and Uhlig (1988).

The operating profit of a particular firm is, however, decreasing in competition. Given the symmetry in research strategies across firms and the symmetry of the demand for the continuum of product lines across the industry, the operating profit of each of the n_{t-1} firms in period t is exactly equal to

$$\frac{1}{n_{t-1}} \overline{\Pi}_t\left(n_{t-1}, v_t, I_t\right).$$

This quantity, *total* operating profits of each firm in the industry is proved in the next proposition to be decreasing in n_{t-1}. This occurs despite the fact that operating profits per product line increases with competition because each firm succeeds in being the "winner" in fewer product-lines.

Both, firm-level and industry-level profits, however increase with the value of total sales in each product line and decrease with the cost of labor. Profits depend positively upon total sales, $P_t(i)Q_t(i)$, because they are a fraction of this and an increase in it, therefore, spurs on research and the resultant technological lead over rivals. Similarly, since firm-level and industry-level research decreases with the unit cost of research labor, w_{t-1}, so do firm and industry operating profits:

$$\frac{1}{n_{t-1}}\overline{\Pi}_t\left(n_{t-1}, v_t, I_t\right) \text{ and } \overline{\Pi}_t\left(n_{t-1}, v_t, I_t\right).$$

As discussed above, the innovation in TFP increases with competition. A measure of this can be derived from (1.1), the factor demand functions of the producing firm in each product line in the industry:

$$k_t(i,j) = \frac{\alpha \cdot I_t}{\gamma_t^*(i,j) \cdot R_t} \qquad \text{and}$$

$$l_t(i,j) = \frac{(1-\alpha) \cdot I_t}{\gamma_t^*(i,j) \cdot w_t}.$$

Given the unit elasticity of the demand function, total sales across product lines ($P_t(i)Q_t(i)$) are constant and proportional to aggregate output y_t. Therefore, the former can replace the latter in these factor demand functions. The inverse of the value shares of factors are therefore proportional to the innovation in TFP at the product, and by integration across product lines, at the industrial level:

$$\int_0^1 \frac{P_t(i)Q_t(i)}{R_t(i)k_t(i)}di \quad \propto \quad \int_0^1 \frac{P_t(i)Q_t(i)}{w_t l_t(i)} \quad \propto \quad \int_0^1 \gamma_t^*(i)di \quad = \quad E\left[\gamma_t^*(i)\right]$$

Since the expected value of the innovation in TFP is increasing in the number of firms that participated in research in the previous period and are now producing in the industry, the inverse of the value shares of factor inputs are also, therefore, predicted by the model to increase with competition, n_{t-1}.

Predictions of the model concerning the implications discussed above are summarized in the following proposition. Note, however, once again the caveat discussed earlier which should be repeated for emphasis. To derive the implications considered above, we have taken the partial derivative of one endogenous variable with respect to another. This is valid only when changes in exogenous variables do not affect the relationship between the number of firms and the other endogenous variables. An example of an exogenous variable that satisfies this criterion is the fixed costs of research. As this varies, only the number of firms conducting research varies directly and any changes in the other endogenous variables are purely due to changes in the number of firms itself.

The first set of inequalities in the proposition below states that while firm-level research decreases with competition, industry-wide research increases. Competition is predicted to have the same effects on firm-level and industry-wide profits, respectively, by the second set of inequalities. The final set of inequalities asserts that our measures of TFP growth at the industrial level increases with competition.

Proposition IV: Let x^* and $n_{t-1}x^*$ (·) denote firm and industry-wide research labor hired in period t-1 respectively, where n_{t-1} denotes the number of firms that engaged in research in period t-1 and are therefore producing in the industry in period t. Similarly, let $\frac{1}{n_{t-1}}\overline{\Pi}_t\left(n_{t-1}, v_t, I_t\right)$ and $\overline{\Pi}_t\left(n_{t-1}, v_t, I_t\right)$ denote *total* firm and industry operating profits in period t. Then the following relationships hold:

1) $\frac{\partial}{\partial n_{t-1}}x^* < 0;$ and $\frac{\partial}{\partial n_{t-1}}\left[n_{t-1}x^*\right] > 0.$

2) $\quad \dfrac{\partial}{\partial n_{t-1}}\left[\dfrac{1}{n_{t-1}}\overline{\Pi}_t\left(n_{t-1},v_t,I_t\right)\right] < 0 ; \quad$ and

$\quad \dfrac{\partial}{\partial n_{t-1}}\left[\overline{\Pi}_t\left(n_{t-1},v_t,I_t\right)\right] > 0$.

3) $\quad \dfrac{\partial}{\partial n_{t-1}}\left[\displaystyle\int_0^1 \dfrac{P_t(i)Q_t(i)}{R_t(i)k_t(i)}di\right] > 0; \quad$ and

$\quad \dfrac{\partial}{\partial n_{t-1}}\left[\displaystyle\int_0^1 \dfrac{P_t(i)Q_t(i)}{w_t l_t(i)}di\right] > 0.$

Furthermore, in the last two inequalities, I_t may be substituted for industrial-level sales.

Proof: See Appendix.

Consider finally, the implication of the model concerning TFP growth for a particular product. Although the measure of TFP growth at the *industrial level*, the *expectation* of $\gamma_t^*(i)$ is non random, for any individual product line, $\gamma_t^*(i)$ is itself a random variable drawn from a distribution function with parameter. $n_{t-1}x^*(n_{t-1},v_t)$. n_{t-1}, however, is itself drawn from N with binomial probability q_{t-1}. If v_t is constant over time then so is q_{t-1}. Therefore $\gamma_t^*(i)$ is identically and independently distributed over time. This implies that if v_t is constant over time then the logarithm of total factor productivity of a particular good: $A_t^*(i)$ is a random walk. In the general equilibrium model in the next chapter v_t is indeed shown to be stationary under reasonable assumptions.

1.5 EMPIRICAL FINDINGS

A preliminary investigation regarding the model's implications concerning the dependence of firm and industry level research inputs and measures of productivity growth on output market concentration has been conducted. The analysis presented below is not to be construed as an empirical check of the model's validity. Neither is it sufficiently rigorous to suggest that the findings should be accepted without conducting further analysis using more thorough econometric techniques. Rather, it is an attempt to review easily available data on a very preliminary basis to determine whether further empirical work regarding the model's implications would be warranted.

Having said that, the results obtained are promising. Although the t-statistics for some of these relationships are not significant enough, most of the relationships are in the direction predicted by the model. It appears that although they may not always be statistically conclusive, our measures of profits and research intensities as well as input demands behave, as functions of a measure of competition, in the manner expected in the model. With regard to total factor productivity growth, the results were more mixed. While the direction of the relationship was as predicted for data at the two digit SIC level, that was not the case for data at the four digit level.

Before proceeding to the data, a discussion of the construction of the independent variable in all the estimated relationships, i.e. the number of firms, is in order. According to the model, the number of firms that compete in research and development in a given period will be exactly equal to the number of firms producing in an industry in the subsequent period. Note that a period is defined as the period of time it takes for a new vintage of technology to be researched, developed and then implemented. Furthermore, in the model, each of these n firms will have exactly (l/n) of the output market share in the production period.

Given that the world consists of a great deal of heterogeneity, the problem becomes one of reconciling the symmetry assumption with the real-world heterogeneity. Following the lead of past authors--see for example Hart (1971) or more recently Richard Levin & Peter Reiss (1984) --we have chosen to take the inverse of the Herfindahl index of concentration as the numbers equivalent in a symmetric world. If indeed the share of the market is symmetric, then the Herfindahl index is indeed equal to (1/n), where n is the number of firms. The construction of the relevant Herfindahl indices is elaborated upon later in this section.

The examination of the data occurred at three levels: at the firm level, at the 2-digit SIC level and at the 4-digit SIC level.

A series of tests was run on data available at the firm level. This data set was derived from the Compustat files by B. Hall and consisted of ten years of observations (1978-1987) of a number of variables for a total of 534 firms. This data set includes a four-digit SIC code for each firm. A subset of this data set, consisting of 189 firms whose SIC code had not changed between 1982 and 1987, the two consecutive Census of Manufacturing years, was derived. The SIC code could have changed simply because of a change in the coding system of the census bureau or because of a real change in the composition of output of the firm in question. In either case, by concentrating only on those firms whose codes had not been changed, it was hoped that the sample consisted mainly of firms facing a stable competitive environment. From the adjusted market value of the firm in 1987 (adjusted for cash holdings and other liabilities to subsidiaries and others) the firm's net capital stock was subtracted. This market value of the firm net of its physical assets was taken to be the variable indicating the discounted future profit stream of the firm. In order to calculate this firm's competitors' number, the SIC code of the firm was matched with the SIC code in the 1987 Census of Manufacturing. The Census lists the shares of output accounted for by the 4, 8, 20, and 50 largest firms and the total number of firms in each 4-digit industry. Using these numbers, a Herfindahl index was created using piece-wise linear approximation. The inverse of the index was taken to be the number of producing firms in the industry in 1987.

The first test was run by creating an industry-equivalent profit measure. This was done by multiplying the number equivalent by the profit measure of the firm. This was then regressed on a constant and the number equivalent. As table I in the appendix shows, the sign is as predicted by the model and the t-statistic is quite significant once corrected for heteroskedasticity. R&D figures for each of the ten years was also available in the data set. If the number equivalent in the output market was n in 1987 then according to the theory, there were n firms competing in R&D in the prior period. Taking the length of the period to be approximately 5 years, R&D expenditures in 1982 at the firm level and at the industry equivalent level (computed by multiplying the number equivalent and the firm level R&D) were individually regressed on a constant and the number of firms. Once again, the signs are as predicted by the theory and while individual firm R&D does decline with the number of competitors, industry R&D increases. The results are in table 1 and while the firm-level t-statistic is quite significant, the industry one is not as significant.

The firm-level R&D regression was repeated with almost identical results for 1983. Finally, 1987 industry investment in capital was regressed on the number equivalent and a constant. The 1987 investment variable was taken to be a proxy for the 1987 capital services cost. Our theory predicts first, that the value of output at the industrial level is constant across intermediate goods and second, that the cost of capital services as a fraction of the value of sales declines with competition. In a cross section regression these two features of the model together then imply that the cost of capital services should decline with competition. Furthermore, as long as investment in new capital is a constant fraction of the total costs of capital services, industry investment should decline with competition because of higher productivity in more competitive industries. The empirical finding is certainly consistent with this although the t-statistic is not very significant, even with a correction for heteroskedasticity.

The second data set was obtained from Jorgenson et. al *Productivity and US Economic Growth*. They construct estimates of the cost of capital services and labor services at approximately the 2-digit SIC level for 51 US industries for 1948 to 1979. They also provide measures of productivity growth at the industrial level. However, their measure of TFP innovations is not applicable under the assumptions of our model because their estimates are based on the assumption of perfect competition. Thus, not only is TFP growth exogenous in their estimates, it is constructed under the implication of the perfectly competitive model where value shares of inputs are equal to their elasticities. In our model that is not the case.

However, their estimates of the cost of capital services can be used because they assume, as we do in our model, that the market for capital services is perfectly competitive. Our implication concerning the growth in industrial total factor productivity was tested with the use of this data on the cost of capital services for 14 industries in 1963, 1967 & 1972 and the numbers equivalent calculated from the census data for these years. The Herfindahl index at the 2-digit level was constructed as a weighted mean of the Herfindahls of the constituent 4-digit industries. Once again, the result is consistent with our theory. The regression result is provided in table 2. For this particular set of tests, total sales were unavailable so the interpretation of I_t as GDP was used in accordance with the aggregate production function interpretation of the source of the demand functions faced by firms.

The same implication was also tested by pooling 4-digit data for each of six 2-digit industries in the census. Value of shipments, labor costs of production workers, cost of new investment (taken as a proxy for cost of capital services) were collected at the 4 digit level. The corresponding Herfindahl indices were also derived from the census data. This was done for the years 1963, 1967 and 1972. For each 2-digit industry, the observations at the 4-digit level were pooled together for the three years and the ratio of the value of shipments to labor costs and to new investments were each regressed on the numbers equivalent calculated from the census data. The results are quite mixed (tables 3&4). Our theory would predict that the coefficient of the numbers equivalent would be positive. For the data on labor costs, the estimated sign was negative for three of the industries. However, the calculated t-statistics were significant for only one of these equations, the one for Primary Metal Industries. For Chemicals and Allied products and Stone, Clay and Glass Products, they were of the right sign and quite significant. The results for the capital series was somewhat similar, of the three estimated with the opposite sign, two were quite insignificant. For Apparel and other Textile Products and Chemicals and Allied products, the coefficients were of the right sign and significant. The problem with the estimates for some of the industries in this set may be that while for the capital series new investments are not good enough as proxies for the cost of capital services, for the labor series adjustment may be somewhat slow so detection of the predicted effects was not quite as strong as for the estimates derived using firm-level data or the exact cost of capital services obtained from the Jorgenson et al. data. The use of value of shipments rather than value added could also have caused some problems.

1.6 CONCLUDING REMARKS

The model constructed in this chapter contains a number of implications concerning the relationship between competition in research and development and productivity growth and factor demands at the firm and industry levels. Some of these have been empirically examined. More empirical work would further contribute to our understanding of the role of competition in driving the technological progress evident in many industries. Empirical examination with a larger sample with other industry and firm-specific variables added would be a worthwhile effort. This would allow us to isolate the role that competition per se plays in the process of technological innovations. A particular additional industry and firm-specific variable of interest is advertising. Advertising is often an important way firms in oligopolistic industries increase firm demands. This could have implications regarding research and development efforts.

In our model we do not examine in detail the nature of the financing of firm R&D expenditures. An explicit modeling of the financing of research and development would also be a worthwhile effort. Firms with poor R&D histories could find themselves unable to compete for outside research funds. The relevance of sustaining a high enough profit level to finance R&D then becomes an issue. Additionally, difficulty in financing may play a selection role in determining the death of firms. This has implications concerning the changing nature of competition and therefore of productivity growth in industries.

II

Research and Development, Physical Capital Formation, and Economic Growth

This chapter analyzes the relative roles played in the process of economic growth by investment in physical capital formation and investment in research and development. A distinguishing feature of research is the possibility of redundancy resulting from a duplication of efforts on the part of individual economic agents, each of whom is motivated by the monopoly rents that accrue to the single innovator who is the first to discover and implement a given technology. Although research increases factor productivity, a diversion of labor from production to research is not costless from a growth perspective. It occurs at the cost of a decline in the production of capital goods, a fundamental engine of economic growth. On the other hand, the increase in total factor productivity resulting from more labor engaged in research depends on how labor is allocated among rival firms and the extent of research duplication by such rivals. The net growth effect of lower capital formation and increased labor in research then depends crucially on the degree of competition and duplication of research in industry. This chapter develops and analyzes a dynamic general equilibrium model where the fractions of the labor force engaged in production and research, firm research intensities, and the degree of competition and duplication are endogenously determined with aggregate prices and output. The impact of changes in the intensity of competition on total factor productivity growth and on the growth rates of capital and output in the short-run and in the long-run are shown to be remarkably different. The intensity of competition is in turn shown to be dependent on income distribution and fiscal policy.

An application of the model lies in explaining why a downsizing of government, a typical ingredient of structural reform, leads to a period of reduced physical capital investment and temporarily lower rates of economic growth. The temporary adverse effects of such reform on growth and capital formation are well documented, e.g. in the World Bank's 1992 report. It is shown in this chapter that reduced taxes lead to a diversion of labor from production to efforts at innovation which causes this phenomenon. It is a result of the short-run tradeoff between innovation and production.

Despite the aforementioned short-run tradeoff, an examination of cross-country data illustrates that economies with a larger fraction of their workforce engaged in research exhibit higher rates of economic growth and capital accumulation (see table 5 in the appendix). Note in particular the correlation of 0.6 between the rate of capital accumulation and the fraction of the workforce engaged in R&D. The implications of the model developed in this chapter are consistent with this observation even when more research goes hand in hand with increased duplication. The chapter shows that the long-run and short-run effects of increased competition on capital accumulation and growth are quite different. While a short-run tradeoff does exist between increased competition in research and capital accumulation, in the long-run no such tradeoff exists. In fact, the long-run rate of capital accumulation is positively related to the amount of competition and duplication *even when competitive forces prevent the implementation of most of the research that takes place*.

Models of endogenous growth in the tradition of Romer (1990), Segerstrom et al. (1990), and Aghion and Howitt (1992) have illustrated the importance of technological innovations in determining the rate of economic growth. These studies abstracted, however, from issues of duplication of research by individual economic agents as is likely in research. Since only a single blueprint of any new innovation is needed, this duplication may at first appear to be wasteful from the point of view of society as a whole as it diverts resources from the production of capital goods. Partial equilibrium models of patent races such as those in Loury (1979), Lee and Wilde (1980) and Reinganum (1982) have emphasized the positive effects on the arrival rate of innovations exercised by increased competition and duplication of research efforts within a single industry. By their very nature, however, these latter papers preclude any analysis of the adverse impact on aggregate economic growth caused by the diversion of productive resources from capital formation to duplicated research efforts on the part of economic agents.

This chapter integrates themes from these two bodies of literature in order to explicitly analyze the effect on the growth rate of the economy of not only increased competition in research but also of the resultant decrease in investment in physical capital formation due to a smaller fraction of labor engaged in production. The steady state rates of growth of aggregate output and capital stock are shown to increase with both competition in research as well as the intensity of research at the firm level. A crucial determinant of both of these variables is shown to be the distribution of income. Any policy that affects income distribution then affects the growth rates of the economy in the long-run.

Unexpected policy changes can, however, have large transitionary effects in the opposite direction from those intended for the long-run. A lowering of taxes on savers in the economy diverts resources to attempts at innovations. The immediate impact is a sharp drop in growth rates with even the possibility of negative growth if the tax reduction is drastic enough. There is also a concurrent drop in investment in physical capital formation. Growth rates rebound subsequently but since current growth rates depend on innovations in total factor productivity as well as on lagged values of past growth rates, this drop in physical capital formation drags down the growth rate of the economy before it eventually reaches and then surpasses previous growth rates. Increased competition in the private sector occurs concurrently with lower growth. It is hoped that this property of the model will prove helpful in explaining some of the features of economies undergoing structural change.

Note that this drop in growth rates does not occur because of a decline in productivity. In fact the rate of productivity growth accelerates relative to the past. However, due to the adverse impact on investment in physical capital, it takes time for the positive effects of increased productivity to outweigh the negative impact on the capital stock. In this regard, the mechanism leading to this transitionary effect is quite different from the one found in Atkeson and Kehoe (1993) where a temporary endogenous decrease in productivity plays the crucial role. This chapter on the other hand shows that increases in productivity can occur concurrently with a decline in the growth rate and the rate of physical capital growth.

The main ingredients of the model constructed in this chapter are as follows. The demographic structure is taken to be that of a two period lived overlapping generations model with constant population. Each agent works only in youth. There exist a large number of intermediate good industries in the economy with each industry producing a number of related products. The output of these industries is combined to produce the aggregate consumption good which can be costlessly transformed into storable capital. The behaviour of firms in each industry regarding research and development and competition in the output market are as discussed in the previous chapter. Within each industry a finite number of firms, endogenously determined, compete separately in the generation of newer vintages of technologies for the production of each and every good in the industry by hiring workers to engage in research and development. Depending on the outcome of the R&D processes, these firms then hire production labor and capital and compete in the output markets of the industries in the following period.

The rest of the chapter proceeds as follows: Section 2 discusses the production sector of the economy and summarizes and examines the general equilibrium implications of the equilibrium research and development process in the intermediate goods sector found in the previous chapter. The decisions faced by economic agents and the definition of dynamic general equilibrium is contained in section 3. The proof of existence of equilibrium is in section 4 of the chapter. Section 5 analyzes the implications of the model regarding income distribution, competition, and growth of output and capital. Section 6 examines the transitionary dynamics due to a decrease in taxes and section 7 concludes.

2.2 PRODUCTION

This section describes the production process in our economy. We use the word production in the usual sense, meaning the transformation of inputs into goods intended for either consumption or to be used as inputs in the production of yet other goods. The "production" of technologies with which inputs are fashioned into outputs is governed by the research and development process analyzed in the previous chapter. Profits garnered from the quasi-monopoly power bestowed upon successful innovators serve as incentives to engage in costly research and development efforts that determines the evolution of the distribution of quantities, prices and technologies in each industry. The equilibrium evolution of these distributions, examined in the previous chapter, are summarized and customized for the purposes of this chapter below.

There exist two production sectors in the economy: the sector that manufactures a composite commodity that serves as both the current consumption good as well as storable capital, and a sector organized into various industries producing a large number of differentiated intermediate products that serve as inputs in the production of the final good. An intermediate good industry is to be thought of primarily as a group of products that share a similar attribute in their production technologies and an associated finite number of firms that have common know-how concerning the improvement of the technology of production for any good within the industry. Each intermediate good industry $j \in [0,1]$ is composed of a continuum of goods or product lines $i \in [0,1]$, and a finite number of producing firms n_j drawn from some underlying universe of potential producing firms in industry j: N_j. We treat N_j as an exogenous parameter of the industry given by historical and institutional factors.

Product lines within an industry have different production technologies. However, within any industry the technologies share enough common attributes that firms possessing experience with the technology of any product line within the industry can compete effectively in the generation of newer vintages of technologies for the production of other product lines in the same industry. In essence, product lines are grouped into industries on the basis of some underlying feature of their production technologies rather than strictly on the basis of any degree of substitutability or some explicit physical properties of the product lines. To retain simplicity, we choose to have product lines within and across industries enter symmetrically into the production function of the final goods. Diagramatically, the structure of the intermediate good production sector can be expressed as:

Figure II
Structure of the Intermediate Good Sector

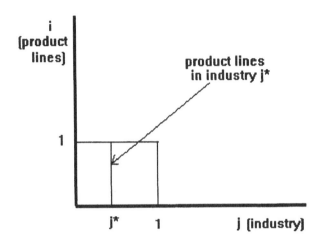

The production function of the composite commodity is given by:

$$y_t = \exp(\int_0^1 \int_0^1 \ln Q_t(i,j) \, di \, dj)$$

where y_t is final good production in period t and $Q_t(i,j)$ is the amount of intermediate good i of industry j used in the production of y_t. The production function is linearly homogeneous in its arguments and we assume that the producers of the final good are price takers in both the input and output markets. We normalize the output price of the final good to be 1 in all periods.

From the cost minimization problem of the final good producer, intermediate good producers face the following demand functions for their products:

$$Q_t(i,j) = \frac{y_t}{P_t(i,j)} \qquad i \,\varepsilon\, [0,1], \; j \,\varepsilon\, [0,1] \qquad (2.1)$$

This demand function is the same as the one faced by firms in the dynamic R&D partial equilibrium model considered in the previous chapter where I_t, the parameter describing the size of demand, is replaced with y_t, aggregate output of the consumption-capital good. $P_t(i,j)$ is the price of product i in industry j. Note that total sales, $P_t(i,j) \cdot Q_t(i,j)$ is constant across product lines and industries and is equal to aggregate output: y_t.

2.2.1 R&D, Industrial Evolution and Duplication

We now summarize and customize the results concerning R&D and output market competition in the intermediate good industries found in the previous chapter for use in a general equilibrium model.

Technologies of production are assumed to be product-line specific and firm-specific. Within each industry, each of the N_j firms in the industry compete in generating the next vintage of technology for each and every product line in the industry. Better technologies discovered through the research process reduce the unit costs of production. The technology of production is:

$$Q_t(i,j) = A_t^s(i,j)k_t^\alpha(i,j)l_t^{1-\alpha}(i,j),$$

where $A_t^s(i,j)$ is the technology accessible to firm s in the production of good i in industry j and k and l are capital and labor. Capital is assumed to depreciate completely.

Firms in one industry do not compete, in either production or in research, in other industries. The patent period is assumed to be one and at the end of the patent period the technology of production governed by the patent becomes freely available for use in production to all N_j firms in the industry. While the patent for a particular technology is in effect, any of the N_j firms have complete access to the technical specifications of the patent and therefore can improve upon it through research and development if they so desire although they cannot currently use it in production.

Research and development in any period entails a three stage decision process. In stage I each of the N_j firms decides whether it wishes to engage in research in that period or not. The cost of choosing to engage in research takes the form of a fixed labor requirement. If it chooses to engage at all, the fixed labor requirement is invariant to the number of product lines within each industry that the firm subsequently conducts research in. Upon engagement, in stage II each firm chooses its research intensity for the technology of each product line for which it chooses to conduct research. We assume no research spillovers between product lines and the decision regarding how much research to conduct for a particular product line is independent of the decision regarding any other product line.

Research intensities are measured in terms of unit labor requirements. The innovation to the existing state-of-the-art technology for a product discovered by a researching firm is a stochastic function of its research intensity. The expected value of the innovation is an increasing and concave function of the research intensity. Thus, each firm conducting research in a particular product line discovers an innovation to the current state-of-the-art technology for that product in stage II of the research period game. Finally, in stage III each firm decides whether to develop its innovation for use in production in the following period or not. For algebraic ease we assume costless development. Finally, in the following period firms compete in Bertrand fashion in the output market for that product. All firms that did not choose to conduct research in the previous period or chose not to develop their discovered innovations will have access to the previous period's state-of-the-art technology as the patent on that technology will have expired. Firms that did conduct research and chose to develop their technologies will have those technologies with which to compete in the output market.

In the equilibrium of this R&D and production game examined in the previous chapter, each of the N_j firms chooses to engage in research in period t with probability q_t. Those that do engage then pay the fixed cost: $w_t \bar{x}$, where $\bar{x}$ is the fixed labor requirement for engaging and w_t is the labor wage rate in period t. Suppose n_j of the N_j firms engage, then each firm chooses the same amount of variable research intensity: x_t^* for each product line in the industry. This intensity, i.e. the magnitude of x_t^* depends only on

$$v_{t+1} = \frac{y_{t+1}}{R_{t+1}w_t},$$

which is to be interpreted as sales per unit variable research costs (R_{t+1} is the interest factor); and on $n_j - 1$, the number of its competitors that also chose to engage in research. The product-line research intensity x_t^* is increasing in v_{t+1} and decreasing in $n_j - 1$. This equilibrium intensity stochastically determines the innovation to the existing state-of-the-art technology discovered by each firm. In stage III of the game only the firm that discovers the largest innovation develops the technology for use in production in the following period. Let $\gamma_{t+1}^*(i,j)$ denote this innovation (for product line i in industry j) and $A_{t+1}^*(i,j)$ the technology that incorporates this innovation to the state-of-the-art technology of period t: $A_t^*(i,j)$. In the following period, as a result of Bertrand competition the firm that discovered the best technological innovation for a given product line in an industry becomes the sole producing firm for that product.

The issue of duplication of research efforts arises in stage III of the R&D process, where all but the "best" innovator choose not to develop their discovered innovations in the technology. Development is forsaken in equilibrium despite the large research costs already incurred. From a general equilibrium viewpoint, this may appear as a waste of resources as the extra labor used in research by firms that never develop their technologies could be put to use in the production sector. This "redundancy" in research also has growth implications as labor is diverted from the production of physical capital, an alternate engine of economic growth.

The price charged by the sole producer of good i in industry j (as a result of Bertrand competition) and its unit cost are:

$$P_{t+1}^*(i,j) = \frac{C(w_{t+1}, R_{t+1})}{A_t^*(i,j)}; \qquad \frac{C(w_{t+1}, R_{t+1})}{A_{t+1}^*(i,j)}.$$

Note that it prices at the unit cost of all of its rivals. The firm's demand for labor and capital which, in combination with the technology, are used to produce the intermediate good are:

$$k_{t+1}(i,j) = \frac{\alpha y_{t+1}}{\gamma^*_{t+1}(i,j) \cdot R_{t+1}}; \quad \text{and}$$

$$l_{t+1}(i,j) = \frac{(1-\alpha)y_{t+1}}{\gamma^*_{t+1}(i,j) \cdot w_{t+1}} \tag{2.2}$$

where α is the elasticity of output with respect to capital. It is shown in the previous chapter that the expectation of the innovation in technology $\gamma^*_t(i,j)$ is increasing in the number of firms that participated in research and in v_{t+1}. Note that despite the fact that only a single firm's technological innovation is implemented, the expected size of that innovation increases as the number of firms that competed in research increases even without any research externalities.

Each firm that chooses to engage in research conducts research in each product line in the industry in a symmetric manner. Therefore each firm that conducts research "wins" the research game for exactly 1 out of n_j of the measure of product lines in the industry and produces 1 out of n_j of the products in the industry in period t+1. Upon producing, the firm does realize a profit, i.e. total sales minus labor and capital costs are positive. However, once the variable and the fixed costs of research are taken into account, the expected profit prior to engagement is exactly equal to zero. This expected profit depends only on q_t, the probability of entry; N_j, the number of firms; and on v_{t+1}, sales per unit research costs:

$$\hat{\Pi}(q_t, N_j, v_{t+1}) \equiv 0 \tag{2.3}$$

For the purposes of this chapter, we will assume that there are exactly the same number of firms in each industry, i.e. $N_j = N, \quad \forall j \in [0,1]$.

Since expected profits from engagement are zero, prior to engaging in research each firm is willing to sign over all rights to future patents, and therefore profits, to any financial intermediary willing to lend the costs of research to the firm. As there is a continuum of industries with the same number of firms in each industry having identical expected profits from engagement as given by (2.3), by the law of large numbers, financial intermediaries collect in present value, profits in period t exactly what they lent to firms in period t-1 to pay for research costs. To raise the funds to be lent for use in research to firms, intermediaries borrow from the young and issue them the claims to operating profits generated in the next period.

Implicit in the above discussion concerning financial intermediation is the condition that the intermediary sign the binding contract with each firm prior to the firm's engagement in research. Renegotiation after the engagement decision but prior to choice of research intensity would void the i.i.d. assumption regarding firm profits.

Total research labor hired by all firms in an industry is the sum of variable research intensity:

$$x_t^* (n_{j-1}, i, j),$$

across researching firms and product lines, and fixed research intensity across researching firms:

$$n_j \left[x_t^* (n_{j-1}, i, j) + \overline{x} \right],$$

This was shown to be increasing in the number of researching firms: n_j in the previous chapter.

2.3 GENERAL EQUILIBRIUM

The demographic structure is taken to be that of a two period lived overlapping generations model with constant population. The size of each generation is normalized to be one. The young have one unit of inelastically supplied labor in youth and live off the returns to previously saved assets in their old age. Labor can either be used in the production of intermediate goods or in the research sector of the economy. We also assume the existence of a government that levies both a wage income tax and an asset income tax. The government uses the proceeds of the tax for either government consumption or for redistribution. Government consumption is assumed not to affect private consumption. A young person born in period t solves the following problem:

$$\text{max} \quad ln\,C_t^t + \beta ln\,C_{t+1}^t$$

(U)   s.t. $C_t^t + S_t = (1 - \tau_w)w_t$

$$C_{t+1}^t = (1 - \tau_a)R_{t+1}S_t$$

where time superscripts denote generations (the period of birth) and subscripts denote periods. τ_w and τ_a are wage and asset tax rates and may be negative in the case of subsidies. Since all agents are identical, the prevailing wage rate in period t, w_t, is the same whether the agent works in production or in research. S_t denotes the savings of the agent in youth and therefore R_{t+1} is the gross rate of return to savings between periods t and t+1. All prices are measured in terms of the consumption/capital good whose price has been normalized to 1 in all periods.

The solution to the utility maximization problem states that the representative agent saves a constant fraction of her after tax wage income:

$$S_t = (1 - \tau_w)\left(\beta \Big/ (\beta + 1)\right) \cdot w_t \qquad (2.4)$$

In period 0, the starting period of the economy, there also exists a generation of agents already in the second period of their lives, each of whom is born with k_0 units of the capital good. Subsequent generations can save either in the form of stored capital, to be rented out to producing firms in their old age, or as claims on the future profits of currently researching firms. As long as the expected profit of firms prior to conducting research is equal to zero, the returns on savings will be the same whether the agent saves in the form of physical capital or by lending to financial intermediaries who in turn lend the funds to research firms in return for claims on any patents.

The economy begins with a distribution of technologies

$$\left\langle A_0^*{}_{(i,j)}\right\rangle; \quad i\,\varepsilon[0,1], \quad j\,\varepsilon[0,1],$$

for the production of each intermediate good. The initial technologies of production are not proprietary and, therefore, are available for use in production by all firms in the economy. An implication of this is that due to free entry, there are no operating profits earned by firms in the initial period. Research conducted beginning with period 0 does, however, imply that operating profits will be positive beginning with period 1.

We assume that in each industry j, the economy begins with N firms capable of undertaking research aimed at improving the technologies of production in the industry. In each period t, including the initial period, these firms make decisions regarding research aimed at improving $A_t^*(i,j)$ in the manner outlined in section 2. Accordingly in each period, each firm decides whether to engage in research or not, how much research to conduct if they do engage, and after the discovery of the technologies, whether to develop them or not.

Given the patent structure, the research technology and Bertrand competition in each industry j where each firm prices according to the technology it possesses, an equilibrium in this economy is defined as follows:

Definition: A Rational Expectations equilibrium is

$$\left(y_t, w_t, R_t, C_t^t, C_{t+1}^t, K_t^s, K_t^d\right)_{t=0}^{\infty} ; \text{ and}$$

$$\left(\sigma_t^*\right)_{t=0}^{\infty} = \left(q_t, (x^*(n_j - 1, v_{t+1}), (develop \text{ iff } \gamma_t^s(i,j) > \gamma_t^{s'}(i,j) \ \forall s' \neq s\right)$$

such that

1) Utility maximization: Given $\left(R_{t+1}, w_t\right)$, $\left(C_t^t, C_{t+1}^t\right)$ solves (U) for each t.
2) Subgame perfect Nash in research and development: For each i, given $\left(y_{t+1}, w_t, R_{t+1}\right)_{t=0}^{\infty}$ and $\left(\sigma_t^{*s'}\right)_{t=0}^{\infty}$, $s' \neq s$, $\left(\sigma_t^{*s}\right)_{t=0}^{\infty}$ solves the profit maximization problem for each research firm s.

3) Output Market Clearing: $y_t = C_t^t + C_t^{t-1} + K_{t+1}^s + g_t$, where K_{t+1}^s is the aggregate capital stock supplied in period t+1 and g_t is government consumption.

4) Capital Market Clearing: $K_t^s = K_t^d$, where K_t^d is the aggregate capital demanded by producing firms in period t.

5) Labor Market Clearing: $L_t^p + L_t^r = 1$, where L_t^p and L_t^r are aggregate labor employed in period t in the production and research sectors respectively.

6) Government budget constraint: $g_t = \tau_w w_t + \tau_a R_t S_{t-1}$

$\left(\sigma_t^{*s} \right)_{t=0}^{\infty}$ is the research firm's strategy concerning engagement in research, how much variable research intensity to target each product line in the industry with, and whether to develop the discovered innovation or not. The first element of σ is the decision regarding engagement, the second the decision regarding variable research input and the third the one regarding development. The equilibrium choice of these is examined in chapter 1 and is also summarized and described in section 2 of this chapter.

2.4 EXISTENCE OF GENERAL EQUILIBRIUM

Our economy is described by two conditions, the output market clearing condition and the zero profit condition for research firms. The latter acts as a no arbitrage condition equating the returns to lending to research firms to storing physical capital.

Consider now the final good market clearing condition in period t that equates the sum of consumption of the two generations plus capital required for the next period to total output:

$$y_t = C_t^t + C_t^{t-1} + K_{t+1}^* + g_t \qquad (2.5)$$

For expositional ease we assume that capital depreciates completely upon use in production.

Since the final good market is perfectly competitive, value of total output has to equal total revenues of the intermediate good sector. The latter quantity is in turn the sum of profits, cost of capital and total production wages in the economy. As current research is financed out of borrowing it is not a claim on *current* total revenue. Noting that the price of the final good is normalized to 1 and substituting for y_t in the above equation, we can rewrite (2.5) in terms of the components of the value of output as:

$$\overline{\Pi}_t^* + R_t K_t^* + w_t L_t^p = C_t^{t-1} + C_t^t + K_{t+1}^* + g_t ; \qquad (2.6)$$

where $\overline{\Pi}_t^*$, and L_t^p denote economy-wide operating profits and total production labor in the intermediate good sector, respectively. Since the first two terms on the left hand-side denote the returns to assets of members of generation t-1, their sum has to exactly equal their consumption C_t^{t-1} and the government's returns from asset income taxation, and we are left with:

$$\tau_a R_t S_{t-1} + w_t L_t^p = K_{t+1}^* + C_t^t + g_t \qquad (2.7)$$

Consider for a moment the case without government. Then both τ_a and g_t are equal to zero and the equation simplifies to:

$$w_t L_t^p = K_{t+1}^* + C_t^t$$

The above equation states that wages received by the young in the *production sector* of the economy has to finance current consumption of that generation as well as the net capital stock (equal to net investment with our assumption of full depreciation) for the next period. If one thinks of each member of the young generation as working part-time in the production sector and part-time in the research sector, it becomes clear as to why it is production wages rather than total wages that have to finance consumption and the capital stock. In this case, effectively the worker is paid for his input into the research process in claims against next period's operating profits. Thus all of his wages earned in the research sector come in the form of savings as claims against future profits. Any consumption or purchase of capital goods then has to come from wages earned in the production sector. This is made clear from substituting the labor market clearing condition, that states that total employment in production and research has to equal one:

$$L_t^p + L_t^r = 1, \tag{2.8}$$

where L_t^r is economy-wide research labor; into (2.7). Rearranging terms and substituting in for the savings decisions of the young as expressed in (2.4) and the government's budget constraint , we have:

$$S_t = (1 - \tau_w)\left(\frac{\beta}{\beta+1}\right) \cdot w_t = L_t^r \cdot w_t + K_{t+1}^*. \tag{2.9}$$

Total savings by the young is equal to total wages earned in the research sector plus investment in physical capital.

The amount of capital needed for production of good (i,j) in a particular period depends on the resolution of the research process in the previous period. The capital requirements for production of good (i,j) in period t+1 is given by (2.2):

$$k_{t+1}(i,j) = \frac{\alpha \cdot y_{t+1}}{\gamma_{t+1}^*(i,j) \cdot R_{t+1}}.$$

This amount declines with the random number $\gamma_{t+1}^*(i,j)$ which denotes the innovation in the total factor productivity of good (i,j). The density function of the innovation depends on total research, which in turn depends on the number of firms that participated in research in industry j, $n_{j,t}$, and on total sales per unit research labor costs v_{t+1}. The average number of firms engaged in research itself increases with the participation rate q_t. Therefore, ultimately the expectation of the inverse of $\gamma_{t+1}^*(i,j)$ is a function of q_t and v_{t+1}.

Due to the symmetry across product-lines, the law of large numbers implies that economy-wide capital requirements in period t is exactly equal to the expectation of the capital requirement of each good (i,j). By the above discussion, economy-wide capital requirements in period t+1 is therefore:

$$K_{t+1}^* = \frac{\alpha \cdot y_{t+1}}{f(q_t, v_{t+1}) \cdot R_{t+1}}; \tag{2.10}$$

where $\dfrac{1}{f(\cdot)}$ is the expectation of the inverse of TFP innovation:

$$\left[\gamma^*_{t+1}(i,j)\right]^{-1}.$$

While an abuse of notation, without any loss in generality $f()$ can be thought of as a measure of economy-wide TFP growth. Note that $f()$ is increasing in q and v. This is because the implemented innovation in each good: $\gamma^*_t(i,j)$ increases with the number of firms participating in research and with v.

Similarly, economy-wide labor allocated to R&D is just the sum across industries of variable research labor and the fixed research support labor. The amount of labor demanded for research in each industry:

$$n_{j,t}\left[x^*_t(n_{j,t},v_{t+1})+\overline{x}\right], \qquad (2.11)$$

depends on the number of participating firms in the relevant industry as well as on total sales per unit research costs. Since industries are symmetric in every way, each firm in each industry engages in research with the same probability q_t. By the law of large numbers, we have economy-wide labor in research as the binomial expectation of (2.11), which is also a function of the rate of entry as well as the measure of potential profits, v_{t+1}. Since industry labor requirement for research increases with the number of firms participating in research and with v_{t+1}, economy-wide research labor: $L^r_t(q_t,v_{t+1})$ is increasing in both of its arguments.

Substituting (2.10) into (2.9), and dividing by the wage rate, we can express the output market clearing condition as:

$$\varphi(q_t,v_t)\equiv(1-\tau_w)\left(\beta/(\beta+1)\right)-L^r_t(q_t,v_{t+1})-\frac{v_{t+1}}{f(q_t,v_{t+1})}\equiv 0 \qquad (2.12)$$

The above and (2.3), the zero expected profit condition in the research sector, are the two equilibrium conditions in our economy. The latter acts as a no-arbitrage condition as it implies that present value of operating profits, to be thought of as returns one period hence to the research workers, is equal to present research wages. Workers in our economy are then indifferent between saving in physical capital and saving by working as either researchers or as research-support staff for firms since they have the same rate of return in present value.

We will look for an equilibrium for our economy, where the two relevant variables, the participation rate of firms q_t and the present value of output to wages ratio,

$$\left(v_{t+1} = \frac{P_{t+1}(i)Q_{t+1}(i)}{R_{t+1}w_t} = \frac{y_{t+1}}{R_{t+1}w_t}\right)$$

are constant over time. The existence of such an equilibrium is stated by the following proposition:

Proposition V: There exists an equilibrium where the participation rate of firms in research and the present value of sales per unit research labor cost in each industry is invariant over time.

proof: See Appendix.

The intuition of the proof can be gained by considering the following diagram:

Figure III
Existence of Equilibrium

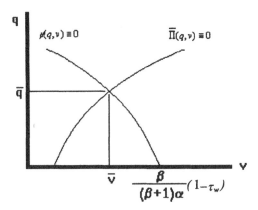

First consider the zero profit condition. Since operating profits are a fraction of total sales, the higher the present value of sales per unit research labor costs, the larger the profit from research upon success in R&D. Therefore profits from research increases with v. In order for expected profits from engagement for an individual firm to equal zero, it then needs to face more competition in research, i.e. a higher participation rate in research for its competitors. This explains the positive slope of the zero profit condition.

An increase in v has two effects on the asset market clearing condition. Since this implies a higher profitability, each firm increases its demand for research labor, i.e. for savings from the young in the form of claims on future operating profits. But more research means a greater growth in TFP and, therefore, demand for physical capital decreases. There are therefore two opposing effects on total demand for assets. Since research increases the productivity of both production labor as well as physical capital, the first effect dominates and, therefore, the effect of a larger v is more demand for assets by each firm. In order to bring demand in line with supply therefore, fewer firms have to participate in research and so the asset market clearing condition is negatively sloped.

2.5 ANALYSIS

From (2.10), total capital stock in period t+1 increases with output in that period and decreases with the interest rate. It is also negatively proportional to the economy-wide increase in total factor productivity in period t+1, a measure of which is provided by $f(q_t, v_{t+1})$:

$$K_{t+1}^* = \frac{(1-\alpha) \cdot y_{t+1}}{f(q_t, v_{t+1}) \cdot R_{t+1}}$$

$f(\cdot)$ is a measure of the average TFP innovation per product line ($\gamma_t^*(i,j)$). This is increasing in both the participation rate of firms in R&D: q_t, and in discounted sales per unit research cost v_{t+1}, the two variables determined by the equilibrium in the previous section. Capital's share of the value of output is decreasing at the economy-wide level as it was at the industrial level with larger q_t and v_{t+1}. The larger the growth in total factor productivity, the larger operating profits in each good, therefore the lower the share of output going to factors of production.

The growth *rate* of aggregate capital stock however, will be seen to be equal to the growth *rate* of aggregate output in the previous period. The latter variable will be shown to be increasing in the economy-wide innovation in TFP. Since this is a function of the innovations at the product-line level, it responds to competition in the same manner as was determined at the industrial level. We will determine below that the growth rate of aggregate output is increasing in total labor allocated to research. This depends positively on the number of firms and on research input per firm, the determinants of which are q_t and v_{t+1}. Thus the rates of growth of output and capital will increase with these variables but with a lag.

Analogous to total capital used, (2.10); total labor employed in the production sector is :

$$L_t^p = \frac{(1-\alpha)\cdot y_t}{f(q_{t-1},v_t)\cdot w_t};\qquad(2.13)$$

Rearranging the above, we derive the share of income earned by the young in each period, the wage to output ratio. This is proportional to the innovation in TFP contributed by the current vintage of technology which is a function of past research, and the current share of labor devoted to research.

$$w_t = c_t \cdot y_t;\qquad c_t = \frac{(1-\alpha)}{f(q_{t-1},v_t)\cdot\left(1-L_t^r\right)}.\qquad(2.14)$$

The present value of sales per unit research costs in period t-1, v_t, is a measure of the inverse of the share of output going to the old in period t. Noting that the young save a constant fraction of their wages, the returns to which in the following period take the form of operating profits and income from capital services, we have:

$$v_t = \frac{y_t}{R_t w_{t-1}} = \frac{\theta\cdot y_t}{\overline{\Pi}_t^* + R_t K_t^*} = \overline{v} \quad \forall t\qquad(2.15)$$

where $\theta = \left(\frac{\beta}{\beta+1}\right)\left(1-\tau_w\right)$ is the fraction of income saved by the young in each period.

Combining the above two equations, we have:

$$y_t = v_t c_{t-1} R_t y_{t-1}, \qquad (2.16)$$

which relates output at present to lagged value of output and the interest rate, and implicitly through the variables v and c to innovations in TFP and the distribution of income.

Consider now the relationship of the interest factor to wages and output. The unit cost of production for the final good producer reflects the costs of each one of the intermediate goods which are his inputs. From the cost minimization problem of the final good producer, we get his unit cost of production in period t to be:

$$\exp\left[\int_0^1 \int_0^1 \ln P_t(i,j)\,di\,dj\right] \qquad (2.17)$$

The price of the final good and therefore due to perfect competition in this sector the unit cost of production of the good, is normalized to be one in all periods. Substituting in for the pricing decisions of the intermediate good producers in period t:

$P_t(i,j) = \dfrac{C(w_t, R_t)}{A^*_{t-1}(i,j)}$, into the above, the relationship of the interest rate

to present wages and past technologies is given by:

$$R_t = a\eta_{t-1}^{-\frac{1}{\alpha}} w_t^{1-\frac{1}{\alpha}}; \qquad (2.18)$$

where a is a constant and $\eta_{t-1} = \exp\left[\int_0^1 \int_0^1 \ln\left(\frac{1}{A^*_{t-1}(i,j)}\right)di\,dj\right]$.

The reason for the appearance of a measure of past technologies in the relationship between interest rates and wages is because each intermediate good producer prices her product at the unit cost of her rivals which is the cost corresponding to usage of vintage t-1 technology. The price of the final good which implicitly contains present costs of factors, therefore contains a measure of *last period's* technologies as well. This lag will play a role in the transition dynamics elaborated upon in the following section.

Substituting (2.18) and (2.14) into (2.16) we derive a first-order difference equation in total output:

$$y_t^{1/\alpha} = v_t c_{t-1} c_t^{1-1/\alpha} a \eta_{t-1}^{-1/\alpha} y_{t-1} \qquad (2.19)$$

Lagging the variables by one time period and defining the growth rate of total output in period t to be $\hat{y}_t = \left(\frac{y_t}{y_{t-1}} \right)$, we derive a first-order difference equation in growth rates from the above:

$$\hat{y}_t^{1/\alpha} = \frac{v_t c_{t-1} c_t^{1-1/\alpha} \eta_{t-1}^{-1/\alpha}}{v_{t-1} c_{t-2} c_{t-1}^{1-1/\alpha} \eta_{t-2}^{-1/\alpha}} \cdot \hat{y}_{t-1} \qquad (2.20)$$

An immediate implication of the equilibrium is that the economy-wide share of labor employed in research, and therefore in production, is constant in each period. Since value of output per unit research costs (v_{t+1}) is constant, operating profits in any particular product line, for a given amount of innovation in total factor productivity, remains the same. As a result, upon engagement in research, each firm hires the same amount of labor for research in each period. Furthermore, with the participation rate of firms in research (q_t) also invariant, although the actual number of firms participating in research in each industry is stochastic, the economy-wide level of competition in research is constant. As both the research input of each firm as well as the number of firms in the economy is constant, so is economy-wide labor input into research.

From our analysis of the innovation in TFP in each period, average growth in TFP depends on the participation rate of firms in research: q_t and in total sales per unit research costs: v_t. Since in equilibrium, both of these and therefore the relative shares of labor engaged in research and production are constant, so is the income share of the young, c_t; i.e. $c_t = \bar{c}$; $\forall t$. Taking account of this, (2.20) simplifies to:

$$\hat{y}_t = \frac{\eta_{t-2}}{\eta_{t-1}} \cdot \hat{y}_{t-1}^{\alpha} \qquad (2.21)$$

Note that since $A_t^*(i,j) = \gamma_t^*(i,j) A_{t-1}^*(i,j)$, we have:

$$\frac{\eta_{t-2}}{\eta_{t-1}} = \exp\left[\int_0^1 \ln\gamma^*_{t-1}(i,j)\,di\,dj\right] \tag{2.22}$$

As the distribution of $\gamma^*_{t-1}(i,j)$ depends only on $q_{t-2} = \overline{q}$ and $v_{t-1} = \overline{v}$; by the law of large numbers η_{t-2}/η_{t-1} is also deterministically constant over time. We, therefore, have a saddle point steady state in the growth *rate* of the economy:

Figure IV
Growth Rate Dynamics

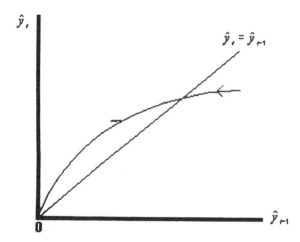

From (2.9), the asset market equilibrium condition, we see that with the fraction of labor in the research sector constant, the capital stock in any given period is a constant fraction of the wage of the young in the previous period:

$$K^*_{t+1} = \left(\theta - L^r_t\right)\cdot w_t$$

Furthermore, by (2.14) wages are a constant fraction of aggregate output. The growth rate of the capital stock is then the growth rate of lagged output.

$$\frac{K_{t+1}^*}{K_t^*} = \frac{y_t}{y_{t-1}}$$

The steady-state value of the latter is given by:

$$= \left(\frac{\eta_{t-2}}{\eta_{t-1}}\right)^{\frac{1}{1-\alpha}}$$

As seen from (2.22) this is a product of the individual (intermediate good-level) innovations in TFP implemented in period t-1, i.e. researched and developed in period t-2. As Grossman and Helpman (1991a) illustrate in a version of their model with physical capital and Lach and Rob (1992) show in a partial equilibrium framework, we see that R&D granger causes capital investment and not the other way around. At least at the firm level, this implication has been empirically substantiated. See for example Hall and Hayashi (1989).

Once again appealing to the law of large numbers, we see that the growth rate of the economy and hence the capital stock is increasing in both the participation rate as well as the measure of the distribution of income, v, both of which are determined simultaneously in equilibrium. Any policy designed to increase the income-share of the young should increase the steady state growth rate of the economy as long as it does not have an adverse impact on the participation rate of firms in research. The effects of such a policy on both the steady state growth rate as well as the transition dynamics are expounded on in the following section. It is found that suddenly and permanently increasing the disposable income of the young, brought about by a reduction in the tax on wage income does increase the steady state growth rate. However, during the transition the economy's growth *rate* will decrease and persist at a relatively lower level for a while before the new steady state is reached.

2.6 TRANSITION DYNAMICS DUE TO TAX CUT

Consider a proportional tax on the old that subsidizes the young. The savings of the young in each period, therefore, increases proportionately with the subsidy. Due to our specification of the utility function, savings is a constant fraction of income when young and, therefore, there are no adverse effects on savings due to substitution effects of the tax. The effect of this is to shift the asset market clearing condition outward. The zero profit condition of firms remains unchanged.

Figure V
Effect of a Tax Cut on Equilibrium

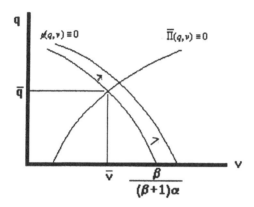

The young save by accumulating physical capital or by working in the research sector of the economy. An increase in their savings implies that the supply of assets increases. The zero profit condition faced by the firms does not change. Therefore, at any level of sales per unit research costs, either more firms can participate in research; or if the same number of firms participate, each can increase its research labor input due to a larger v. In equilibrium both of these happen and therefore both v and q increase. As discussed above, this implies that the steady-state growth rate of the economy improves.

A decrease in income taxes that were being used to finance government consumption has exactly the same effects. A change in asset income taxes, i.e. taxes on the old, without a change in taxes on the young however has no effects on the growth rate of the economy as the asset market clearing condition and the zero profit condition remain unchanged. The fact that wage income taxes are growth retarding in overlapping generation economies is in itself not a new result. Jones and Manuelli (1992) and Uhlig and Yanagawa (1992) both illustrate this. What this chapter does is to highlight an additional mechanism by which this occurs, namely through a lowering of the intensity of competition in R&D. This chapter also provides an additional result showing that a decrease in taxes can *temporarily* decrease the growth rate.

A decrease in wage taxes shifts labor towards more research. If the tax decrease is sudden and unexpected, this implies a lowering of output produced as there are now fewer workers in the production sector. It is this transitory change that provides the mechanism for a temporary decline in growth rates. Since capital is an input in the production process, the growth rate of the economy exhibits persistence, reflecting changes in the capital stock that occur during transition. This persistence in growth rates provides the mechanism for a prolonged period of relatively lower growth rates before exceeding the rate of growth in effect before the tax cut.

To examine the transitional dynamics of an economy where the tax on the young is lowered, suppose the tax decrease on the young is announced and implemented in period t. The effect of that on the equilibrium allocation of resources in the economy is as described above, an outward shift in the asset market clearing condition resulting in an increase in equilibrium sales per unit research labor costs: $v_{t+1} > v_t$ and an increase in the participation rate of firms: $q_t > q_{t-1}$. Thereafter, as long as the tax decrease is permanent, both variables remain at their newer and higher levels. Consider (2.19), the difference equation in total output:

$$y_t^{1/\alpha} = v_t c_{t-1} c_t^{1-1/\alpha} a \eta_{t-1}^{-1/\alpha} y_{t-1} \qquad (2.23)$$

The variables v_t, and

$$c_{t-1} = \frac{(1-\alpha)}{f(q_{t-2}, v_{t-1}) \cdot (1 - L_{t-1}^r)}$$

are determined in period t-1 or earlier. c_t itself is a function of q_{t-1} and v_t, variables determined in period t-1 as well as a function of the period t share of labor in research. In period t, the effect of an increase in q_t and v_t, due to the new equilibrium is to increase the fraction of the labor engaged in research in *that period* and therefore increase c_t. The magnitudes of all the other variables that form the coefficient of the past level of output in (2.23) were, as discussed above, determined in the past according to the equilibrium then in effect.

Substituting in for c_{t-2}, c_{t-1} and c_t in the difference equation in growth rates (2.20), we get:

$$\hat{y}_t^{1/\alpha} = \left(\frac{L_n^p}{L_0^p}\right)^{\frac{1-\alpha}{\alpha}} \left(\frac{\eta_{t-1}}{\eta_{t-2}}\right)^{-1/\alpha} \hat{y}_{t-1},$$

where L_0^p and L_n^p are labor in production in the old and new equilibria respectively. As is clear from this, the output of the economy relative to what it would have been without the change drops suddenly. The sudden effect of an increase in the fraction of the labor force in research is to decrease the fraction of the labor force in production. Since technologies in effect in period t as well as the capital stock were determined by the previous period, the effect is a lower level of output than would have been produced if the fraction of labor in research had not increased.

The following period, the new larger values of v_{t+1} and c_t exert a positive effect on the growth rate. Equation (2.20) forwarded one period is:

$$\hat{y}_{t+1}^{1/\alpha} = \frac{v_{t+1}}{v_t} \cdot \frac{L_0^p}{L_n^p} \cdot \left[\frac{f(q_t, v_{t+1})}{f(q_{t-1}, v_t)}\right]^{\frac{1-\alpha}{\alpha}} \cdot \left[\frac{\eta_t}{\eta_{t-1}}\right]^{-1/\alpha} \cdot \hat{y}_t \qquad (2.24)$$

Note that there is no change in the values of η_t yet as these were determined as part of the old equilibrium. They are the results of research conducted in periods t-1 and earlier. Therefore, in period (t+1), the economy rebounds strongly relative to the (lower) growth rate in period t. Thereafter, all the variables remain the same except for the general level of technology η_t, improvements on which are now higher because of larger participation rates and research efforts per firm due to higher v. The economy then grows according to:

$$\hat{y}_\tau = \frac{\eta_{\tau-2}}{\eta_{\tau-1}} \cdot \hat{y}_{\tau-1}^\alpha; \; \tau = t+3, \ldots,$$

with $\eta_{r-2}\big/\eta_{r-1}$ constant in each period but higher than before the policy change. Since the growth rate of capital is the same as the growth rate of output with a one period lag, the former variable follows the same path of transition as the latter.

Graphically, the effect can be expressed as follows.

Figure VI
Transition Dynamics

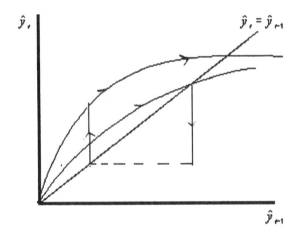

As can be seen, depending on the magnitude of the original drop in output, the economy may take some time before it reaches the growth rates seen in the past. Although growth through larger innovations in total factor productivity persist from period t+1 onwards, the decline in the capital stock due to lower investments in period t drags down the growth rate of the economy for a period of time. Eventually the economy reaches and then surpasses the rates of growth seen prior to the transition.

The mechanism behind the effects of the transition is as follows: R&D has an effect on total factor productivity with a one period lag. Innovations discovered this period are implemented only in the following period. The young save through physical capital accumulation and by working in the R&D sector. An unforeseen and permanent increase in disposable income due to lower taxes increases the savings of the young and leads to an increase in competition and research demand by firms. Thus more workers now work in the research sector relative to the past and given the existing levels of technology and capital stock in period t, the corresponding decrease in the size of the producing labor force implies a drop in current output. Since investment in physical capital is proportional to output, capital for the following period also declines. Therefore, although larger innovations in total factor productivity persist from then on, the lowered amount of capital drags down the growth rate for a period of time.

Increases in total factor productivity occur during the entire transition period. The mechanism leading to temporarily lower rates of growth is therefore quite different from Atkeson and Kehoe (1993). "Information capital" concerning the matching of managers to technologies plays the primary role in their analysis. The drop in output and physical capital investment in their model occurs because of a temporary decline in productivity due to a decrease in information capital caused by an acceleration in the adoption of new technologies. The evolution of the distribution of technologies from which adoption occurs is taken to be exogenous and a reforming economy is primarily characterized by its increased ability to adopt technologies from this evolving distribution. In contrast, the present model is of an entirely closed economy with endogenous technological innovations about which there is no uncertainty once the initial discovery is complete. Furthermore, reform is characterized primarily as a downsizing of the government sector. Reform being a complex process, both of these characterizations are probably valid, and therefore both of these effects, alone or in tandem, provide explanations for the observed phenomena.

2.7 CONCLUDING REMARKS

In this chapter a model of economic growth has been developed that explicitly incorporates differences in physical capital investment and investment in research and development. Competition in R&D in our model accounts for both the evolution of industry as well as growth in total factor productivity at the industrial and aggregate levels. Increased competition is shown to have a positive impact on TFP growth. However, increased competition, with the associated redundancy in research efforts, comes at a cost of less physical capital formation. Income distribution and fiscal policy are shown to affect both the intensity of competition and research input by individual firms. It is shown that in the steady state more competition and less production of capital goods does not imply a lower rate of growth for either output or capital. However, in the short-run policy changes that move the economy to a steady state with a higher rate of growth are shown to lead to the exact opposite, with a prolonged period of lowered growth before the growth rate recovers and then surpasses its previous levels. This effect is proposed as one explanation of the behaviour of investment and growth in economies undergoing structural reform.

The general equilibrium considered in this chapter had v_t being constant in all periods except for jumps exhibited when the tax rate changed due, inter alia, to changes in the composition of government revenue. An implication of this feature is that for the model developed in the previous chapter, the log of total factor productivity would be a random walk. Changes in the composition of government revenue would, however, impact upon the expected innovation in technologies of all products in the economy through its effect on v_t.

Government revenue, in the model developed in this chapter, is assumed to go towards government consumption. While this highlights the temporary negative effect on the growth rate of decreasing the tax burden on savers, it is not entirely realistic. Allowing for government investment would enrich the model significantly. Insights can be gained concerning the optimal allocation of government funding towards consumption and investment in physical capital formation during periods of reform. If government steps up investment in physical capital formation at the same time that it lowers the tax burden of savers, the steep decline in production may be averted. The same may be true with subsidies to the private formation of physical capital.

We have considered Hicks neutral technical progress. Allowing for technology to improve the productivity of only labor or of only capital may contribute to furthering our understanding of the macroeconomic relationship between labor in production and labor in research and development.

Firms in our model finance R&D through borrowing. Financial intermediation is considered to be costless and the results of the research undertaken are considered to be fully verifiable by lenders. While useful abstractions for the purpose of this chapter, the incorporation of a richer role for financial intermediation may be a worthwhile endeavor. It may shed light on how financial development eases credit constraints and thereby affects productivity growth. At the industrial level, ongoing relationships between financial intermediaries and firms may affect the process of industrial evolution.

These are all avenues for productive future research. The insights gained from the present model are straightforward enough that these avenues may be easily explored in the future using versions of this model.

III

The Dissemination of New Knowledge and Economic Growth

The diffusion of knowledge is an important engine of long-run economic growth. Newly created knowledge contributes to economic growth through two channels. First of all, it enables the creation of newer and higher quality goods and services and thereby increases output directly. In addition, if the knowledge thus created or discovered is widely diffused, it acts as an input in the creation of yet newer and better goods. The rate and speed of the dissemination of knowledge is, therefore, a crucial determinant of the rate of economic growth.

Recent models of economic growth (Romer, 1990 & Aghion & Howitt 1992) have contributed to our understanding of how the introduction of new intermediate goods, or of goods of higher quality and efficiency, contribute to increased output. However, the continual introduction of such goods in these models is made possible by an externality in the generation of knowledge where each vintage of knowledge costlessly and automatically increases the productivity of future researchers. This amounts to assuming that the new knowledge diffuses instantaneously and costlessly in a form where it is useful in the creation of yet newer and better goods.

This chapter argues that with large private costs to adopt and adapt existing knowledge for use in research, such diffusion is unlikely to occur and hence a tax-subsidy system is required if knowledge is to be disseminated. With costly adoption and no active dissemination, the existence of strong intertemporal increasing returns of knowledge to society, per se, is insufficient to sustain growth without active efforts at diffusion.

Governments have long recognized the economic benefits of disseminating knowledge. They often subsidize not only innovation, i.e. the creation of new knowledge, but also its imitation and adoption, i.e. diffusion of such knowledge. As Rustichini and Schmitz (1991) cite, agriculture is a prime example of government subsidizing both innovation and imitation. In addition, the financing of public schools through property taxes, as in the United States, is a more general example of government-financed dissemination of knowledge. Various grants and subsidies offered for the dissemination of new knowledge through publication and the broadcast media is another channel through which government encourages the dissemination of new knowledge.

We also identify an additional incentive for government to disseminate knowledge in order to encourage economic growth. The incentive to undertake efforts at innovation is motivated by the monopoly rents that accrue to the successful innovator. However, in the presence of costly imitation, the expiration of a patent by itself does not result in the loss of monopoly power. This persistence of monopoly tends to divert resources away from the creation of new intermediate goods, the direct reason for increased output in these models of economic growth. Essentially, the persistence of monopolies tends to transfer income from young workers and savers to retired dis-savers and hence retards the process of creating new knowledge. The negative impact of such a transfer of income is identified by Jones & Manuelli (1992), and Chou and Shy (1993) discuss the crowding out effects of long duration of patents that effectively results in such a transfer. Governments, therefore, have an additional incentive to disseminate knowledge, once the patent period is over, in order to dilute monopoly power and hence divert savings into growth generating areas.

The fact that the costs of imitation are high is verified by Mansfield, Schwartz and Wagner (1981). In their sample of new innovations that were imitated, the average cost of imitation was 65% of the costs of innovation. Given such high costs, the diffusion of knowledge is unlikely to occur in the presence of strong output market competition and hence a role for public support of dissemination is called for. The question then becomes: what considerations need to be taken into account in determining the level of public intervention in disseminating previously created knowledge? This is the topic this chapter attempts to address.

The rest of the chapter proceeds as follows: Section 2 constructs the basic work-horse model used in the chapter, it is an overlapping generations version of a model where growth occurs through the creation of new intermediate goods. Section 3 argues that an externality feature of knowledge is the engine behind the continual introduction of new intermediate goods in the model thus constructed. It is argued there that new knowledge would need to be publicized in order to sustain growth. A discussion of the role played by the persistence of monopoly in retarding growth is also contained in the section. Section 4 introduces government into the model and examines how that modifies the growth process. Section 5 considers the optimal level of governmental involvement in the dissemination process and section 6 concludes.

3.2 THE BASIC MODEL

This section describes an overlapping generations version of the growth model where the source of growth is an increase in the variety of intermediate goods used in the production of the final good as in Romer (1980) and Grossman and Helpman (1990). The constant increase in variety, and therefore in output, in the model will be shown to be caused by an externality in the research and development process. At the time of discovery, an increase in the stock of knowledge costlessly and permanently increases the productivity of all research workers regardless of who it is that actually discovers the new knowledge. In other words, the dissemination of new knowledge is assumed to be complete and costless. This new knowledge contributes to the productivity of research workers. However, the use of the knowledge in the production of intermediate goods is governed by a patent system that protects the successful innovator *completely* against imitation in production during the patent period and thereby rewards her with monopoly rents. The patent period is fixed exogenously. If and when the patent period expires, the monopolist's profits cease to be positive if imitation in production occurs. The expiration of a patent per se however does not cause increased research productivity as all the knowledge embodied in the patent has already disseminated when the knowledge is first discovered

The demographic structure is taken to be that of two period lived overlapping generations with constant population. The size of each generation is normalized to be one. The young have one unit of inelastically supplied labor in youth and in old age live off the returns to assets accumulated in youth. Labor can either be used in the production of intermediate goods or in the research sector of the economy. A young person born in period t solves the following problem:

$$\max \quad ln\ C_t^t + \beta\ ln\ C_{t+1}^t$$
$$\text{s.t.} \quad C_t^t + S_t = w_t$$
$$C_{t+1}^t = R_{t+1}S_t$$

where time superscripts denote generations (the period of birth) and subscripts denote periods. Since all agents are identical, the prevailing wage rate in period t, w_t, is the same whether the agent works in production or in research. S_t denotes the savings of the agent in youth and R_{t+1} is the gross rate of return to savings between periods t and t+1. The price of the consumption good is normalized to be 1 in all periods. From the first order condition of the problem, we derive the following relations:

$$\frac{C_{t+1}^t}{C_t^t} = \beta \cdot R_{t+1}$$

$$S_t = \delta \cdot w_t = \left(\frac{\beta}{(1+\beta)}\right) \cdot w_t \qquad (3.1)$$

The first equation gives us the relationship between the interest rate and the ratio of consumption when young and consumption when old. The second equation states that the young save a constant fraction of their wage income.

The production function of the composite consumption good is given by:

$$y_t = \left[\int_0^{n_t} Q_t^\alpha{}_{(i)} \, di \right]^{1/\alpha}$$

where y_t is final good production in period t, n_t is the measure of intermediate goods that are produced that period and $Q_{(i)}$ is the amount of intermediate good i used in the production of the final good. All goods are assumed to be perishable and hence non-storable. Given n_t, the production function exhibits constant returns to scale in its inputs and we assume that the producers of the final good are price takers in both the input and output markets.

The final good producers solve the following problem:

$$\min \quad \int_0^{n_t} P_t{}_{(i)} Q_t{}_{(i)} \, di$$

$$\text{s.t.} \quad y_t = \left[\int_0^{n_t} Q_t^\alpha{}_{(i)} \, di \right]^{1/\alpha},$$

where $P_{t(i)}$ is the price of intermediate good i. From the cost minimization problem, we derive the (conditional) demand function for the intermediate goods:

$$Q_t{}_{(i)} = \frac{y_t P_t^{1/(1-\alpha)}{}_{(i)}}{\left[\int_0^{n_t} P_t^{\alpha/(\alpha-1)}{}_{(i)} \right]^{1/\alpha}}.$$

The unit cost of the final good producer is given by:

$$\left[\int_0^{n_t} P_t^{\alpha/(\alpha-1)}{}_{(i)} \right]^{(\alpha-1)/\alpha},$$

which equals one because of the normalization of the final good price. The demand for intermediate good i then simplifies to:

$$Q_t{}_{(i)} = y_t \cdot P_t^{1/(1-\alpha)}{}_{(i)} \tag{3.2}$$

Each intermediate good is produced by a monopolist who has exclusive rights governed by a patent for the technology of production for that good. We will assume that the patent period is infinite for the time being and will later show that the results would be unchanged with finite patent lengths but costly imitation. Each unit of labor can produce one unit of an intermediate good. In period t, each of the monopolist producers of the n_t intermediate goods therefore solves the following problem:

$$\max \ P_t(i)Q_t(i) - w_tQ_t(i),$$

subject to the conditional demand function (3.2). The price, quantity and profit of each of the monopolists are as follows:

$$P_t(i) = \frac{w_t}{\alpha}, \tag{3.3}$$

$$Q_t(i) = y_t \cdot \left[\frac{w_t}{\alpha} \right]^{1/(\alpha-1)} \tag{3.4}$$

$$\pi_t(i) = (1-\alpha)y_t \left[\frac{w_t}{\alpha} \right]^{\alpha/(\alpha-1)} \tag{3.5}$$

The economy also has a research sector where labor is employed in the creation of blueprints for the production of new intermediate goods. Once the blueprint for a new intermediate good is discovered, the rights to the production of that good, which enjoys patent protection, are sold to a single producer who then derives an infinite stream of profits as given by (3.5):

$$\sum_{\tau=1}^{\infty} \frac{\pi_{t+\tau}}{\prod_{s=1}^{\tau} R_{t+s}}$$

Since there is competitive bidding by producers for the rights to the patent governing the production of an intermediate good, the price that the monopolist pays to the researcher is exactly equal to the discounted value of the future stream of monopoly profits. There is a one period lag between the discovery of a new intermediate good and the start of the production of that good. In period t, therefore, a research firm chooses its output--new blueprints, and the units of labor to create these blueprints in order to maximize the present value of the infinite stream of future profits. Let

$$V_t = \sum_{\tau=1}^{\infty} \frac{\pi_{t+\tau}}{\prod_{s=1}^{\tau} R_{t+s}}$$

Research firms then solve:

$$\max \quad (n_{t+1} - n_t)V_t - w_t x_t, \tag{3.6}$$

where $(n_{t+1} - n_t)$ is the measure of new intermediate good blueprints created and x_t is the amount of labor employed in research. Blueprint creation is governed by the following deterministic "production" function:

$$\Delta n_{t+1} = (n_{t+1} - n_t) = \lambda n_t x_t, \quad \lambda > 0 \tag{3.7}$$

Labor's productivity in research increases with the stock of knowledge in the economy as embodied in the "research production function" by the number of intermediate goods currently in production n_t. There is, therefore, a positive externality in the process of knowledge creation, where the larger the stock of current knowledge: n_t, the more productive the research process is. Due to free entry into research the profit of the research firm is driven to zero and the value of the patent of a new good is given by:

$$V_t = \frac{w_t}{\lambda n_t} \tag{3.8}$$

Note that this is due to the free entry condition in the research sector, or in other words is a partial equilibrium determination of the value of the future stream of profits. In the final analysis, V_t depends on the value of future profits, which in turn depend on future values of the wage rate and aggregate output, and on present and future interest rates:

$$\sum_{\tau=1}^{\infty} \frac{\pi_{t+\tau}}{\prod\limits_{s=1}^{\tau} R_{t+s}},$$

$$\pi_{t}(i) = (1-\alpha)y_{t}\left[\frac{w_{t}}{\alpha}\right]^{\alpha/(\alpha-1)}$$

Output, wages and interest rates are all determined in general equilibrium and using the values determined for these variables it will be explicitly shown at the end of this section that, indeed,

$$\sum_{\tau=1}^{\infty} \frac{\pi_{t+\tau}}{\prod\limits_{s=1}^{\tau} R_{t+s}} = \frac{w_{t}}{\lambda n_{t}}.$$

We now consider the general equilibrium that will determine the levels of output, wages and interest rates as functions of the primitives and of the number of intermediate goods in existence. The rate of evolution of the number of goods will, in turn, be shown to be a function of the primitives as well.

The young in the model work in either research, producing blueprints for new intermediate goods, or in production. In each period they save a constant fraction of their wage by acquiring the patent rights to the production of intermediate goods. These patent rights may be for intermediate goods previously created or for those created in the current period. In old age, they enjoy the period monopoly rents due to the patent holder and sell the patent rights for future production to the then current young. Consumption by the young is a fraction of their wage income and consumption when old of the generation born in period t, i.e. during period t+1 is, therefore, equal to the period monopoly profits of the n_{t+1} intermediate goods plus the resale value of the patent rights to these goods.

The total wage bill for the production of an intermediate good is given by:

$$w_{t}l_{t}(i) = w_{t}Q_{t}(i) = w_{t} \cdot y_{t}\left[\frac{w_{t}}{\alpha}\right]^{1/(\alpha-1)}$$

where $l_t(i)$ is labor used in the production of good i in period t and the equalities involve the substitution of the production decision of the intermediate good producers as given by (3.4). Thus the total wage bill plus period profits (3.5) per intermediate good is given by:

$$w_t l_t(i) + \pi_t(i) = y_t \cdot \left[w_t \big/ \alpha \right]^{\alpha/(\alpha-1)} \tag{3.9}$$

Similarly, after substituting the pricing decision of the intermediate good producers, (3.3), into the unit cost (normalized to 1) of the final good producer, we get:

$$\int_0^{n_t} P_t^{\alpha/(\alpha-1)}(i) \, di = \int_0^{n_t} \left(w_t \big/ \alpha \right)^{\alpha/(\alpha-1)} = 1 \tag{3.10}$$

Integrating (3.9) and using (3.10), we then derive:

$$n_t \left[w_t l_t + \pi_t \right] = y_t \tag{3.11}$$

where l_t and π_t are the (symmetric) labor required and profit per intermediate good.

Since consumption of the young in period t is equal to $C_t^t = (1-\delta)w_t$ and consumption of the old is equal to $C_t^{t-1} = n_t \pi_t + n_t V_t$, substituting these in the output market clearing condition:

$$y_t = C_t^t + C_t^{t-1} ,$$

we derive:

$$n_t w_t l_t + n_t \pi_t = (1-\delta)w_t + n_t \pi_t + n_t V_t \tag{3.12}$$

Substituting the labor market condition that states that the sum of total labor in research: x_t and total labor in production $n_t l_t$ has to equal one into the above, and rearranging terms, we obtain:

$$\delta w_t = x_t w_t + n_t V_t , \tag{3.13}$$

which states that the entire savings of the young is either as labor in research , $x_t w_t$ --where they get paid the value of their wage in patent rights to the new intermediate goods they create--or as the purchase of preexisting patents from the old.

Finally, substituting in the research labor: $x_t = \Delta n_{t+1}/\lambda n_t$ and the value of the patents:

$$V_t = {}^{w_t}\!\!\big/\!_{\lambda n_t}$$

into (3.13), we obtain the equilibrium growth rate of intermediate goods as a function of labor's productivity in research λ and of the savings rate δ:

$$\lambda\delta = \frac{n_{t+1}}{n_t}, \qquad (3.14)$$

We therefore have a difference equation in n, the measure of intermediate goods. We will assume that λ is sufficiently large so that $\lambda\delta > 1$. This amounts to assuming that some research gets done every period.

Now consider a finite patent period, say of one. In this case, exclusive use of the technology in production is only allowed for one period. However, in the presence of price competition and even the slightest cost of imitation, after the patent period expires no other firm will imitate any of the producing firms and compete with them in the output market for intermediate goods. Under Bertrand competition, the price that would prevail if imitation does occur would exactly equal the unit cost of production and thus there would be no profits. Hence it is sub-optimal for any firm to undertake costly imitation. In effect, due to the cost of imitation, the producing firm would enjoy the benefits of infinite patent protection even when the patent formally expires after one period. Our results so far would then remain unchanged.

We now determine the equilibrium value of output, wages and the interest rate as functions of the number of intermediate goods and of primitives. The period t output of the final consumption good is given by:

$$y_t = \left[\int_0^{n_t} Q_t^\alpha (i)\,di\right]^{1/\alpha} = \left[\int_0^{n_t} l_t^\alpha (i)\,di\right]^{1/\alpha} = l_t n_t^{1/\alpha} \qquad (3.15)$$

where l_t is the (symmetric) production labor per intermediate good. From the labor market clearing condition, we have: $n_t l_t = 1 - x_t$. However, total research labor, x_t, is given by (3.7) and equals $\Delta n_{t+1}/\lambda n_t$. The latter term is constant and equal to $\delta - \frac{1}{\lambda}$ and therefore production labor per intermediate good in period t is given by:

$$l_t = \frac{1 + \lambda(1 - \delta)}{\lambda n_t} .$$ (3.16)

Substituting for production labor in (3.15), we get output as a function of the number of intermediate goods:

$$y_t = n_t^{\frac{(1-\alpha)}{\alpha}} \cdot [1 + \lambda(1 - \delta)]/\lambda .$$ (3.17)

Thus, in equilibrium, aggregate output is a function of the number of intermediate goods, of λ and of the savings rate, δ. The growth rate of output is therefore:

$$\frac{y_{t+1}}{y_t} = \left(\frac{n_{t+1}}{n_t}\right)^{\frac{1-\alpha}{\alpha}}$$

Consider now the determination of the equilibrium wage rate. Since one unit of labor produces one unit of an intermediate good and from the producer's decision (3.4),

$$Q_t(i) = y_t \cdot \left[\frac{w_t}{\alpha}\right]^{\frac{1}{(\alpha-1)}} ,$$

we have from (3.16): $\qquad \dfrac{1 + \lambda(1 - \delta)}{\lambda n_t} = y_t \cdot \left[\frac{w_t}{\alpha}\right]^{\frac{1}{(\alpha-1)}} .$

Finally, substituting in for the equilibrium output (3.17), we derive equilibrium wages as a function of the number of intermediate goods:

$$w_t = \alpha \cdot n_t^{\frac{(1-\alpha)}{\alpha}}$$ (3.18)

The growth rate of wages is then the same as the growth rate of output.

Consider now the derivation of the equilibrium level of profit per intermediate good, π_t. Restating (3.11) which states that value of output equals profit plus labor costs:

$$n_t\left[w_t l_t + \pi_t\right] = y_t,$$

and substituting in (3.16), (3.17) and (3.18) into the above and rearranging terms we obtain:

$$\pi_t = (1-\alpha)\frac{y_t}{n_t} \qquad (3.19)$$

which gives us equilibrium profit as a function of output which, in turn, is a function of the number of intermediate goods.

Finally, we determine the equilibrium interest rate from the consumer's first order condition:

$$\frac{C_{t+1}^t}{C_t^t} = \beta \cdot R_{t+1}.$$

Substituting in (3.8), (3.18) and (3.19) into the consumer's consumption decisions in youth and old age, we have:

$$R_{t+1} = \frac{1 + (1-\alpha)\lambda(1-\delta)}{\alpha\lambda\delta}\frac{w_{t+1}}{w_t}, \qquad (3.20)$$

or substituting in for the growth rate of wages which equals the growth rate of output:

$$R_{t+1} = \frac{1 + (1-\alpha)\lambda(1-\delta)}{\alpha\lambda\delta}(\lambda\delta)^{\frac{1-2\alpha}{\alpha}}.$$

We see that the interest rate depends on λ, the substitutability of intermediate goods in the production of the final good, α, and on the savings rate δ. It is, furthermore, constant over time.

Finally, as indicated above, we show that in equilibrium the discounted value of future profits:

$$\sum_{\tau=1}^{\infty}\frac{\pi_{t+\tau}}{\prod_{s=1}^{\tau}R_{t+s}}$$

does indeed equal $\frac{w_t}{\lambda n_t}$ as determined by free entry into research.

Substituting in for $\pi_{t+\tau}$ and R as given by (3.19) and (3.20) and using the growth rate of output and of the number of intermediate goods:

$$y_{t+1} = \left(\frac{n_{t+1}}{n_t}\right)^{\frac{1-\alpha}{\alpha}} y_t, \text{ and } n_{t+1} = (\lambda \delta) n_t, \text{ respectively,}$$

we obtain:

$$\sum_{\tau=1}^{\infty} \frac{\pi_{t+\tau}}{\prod_{s=1}^{\tau} R_{t+s}} = (1-\alpha) \frac{y_t}{n_t} \sum_{s=1}^{\infty} \left(\frac{\alpha}{1+(1-\alpha)\lambda(1-\delta)}\right)^s$$

$$= (1-\alpha) \frac{y_t}{n_t} \frac{\alpha}{1+(1-\alpha)\lambda(1-\delta)-\alpha}.$$

Finally, using (3.17) and (3.19) to substitute wages for aggregate output, we have:

$$\sum_{\tau=1}^{\infty} \frac{\pi_{t+\tau}}{\prod_{s=1}^{\tau} R_{t+s}} = \frac{w_t}{\lambda n_t}.$$

3.3 EXTERNALITIES AND MARKET POWER

This section examines the roles played in determining the growth rate in the basic model presented above by: 1) the externality in research, and 2) the effective existence of perpetual monopoly power derived from inventing a new intermediate good. The possibility for government to affect the growth rate through manipulation of these channels is discussed.

The source of continued investment in the generation of new intermediate goods in the model above is the positive intertemporal externality caused by increased knowledge. The extent of this externality determines the growth rate of the economy.

The existence of perpetual monopoly power on the other hand, ensures that the blueprint of a good once created will forever have positive value. This monopoly power, therefore, negatively affects the creation of new intermediate goods in the economy by diverting the savings of the young towards purchasing pre-existing blueprints rather than creating new ones.

3.3.1 Knowledge in the Public and Private Domains

Under the case where knowledge created by a given generation does not pass costlessly to members of future generations and the active acquisition of sufficient amounts of previously created knowledge by an individual is ruled out because it is too costly, the productivity of workers in research would remain constant at λ, i.e.

$$\Delta n_{t+1} = \lambda x_t \text{ and } V_t = \frac{w_t}{\lambda}.$$

If research did occur in period t, then substituting these into (3.13), we would have the period t market clearing condition (3.14):

$$\lambda \delta = n_{t+1} > n_t$$

In the following period, i.e. in t+1, if research were to be undertaken again, $\lambda \delta = n_{t+2}$. This, however, is impossible if there is positive research, i.e. if $n_{t+2} > n_{t+1}$. Thus, at most one period of research would occur and then growth in variety as well as in output would cease.

The assumption in the basic model that research productivity of generation t is λn_t, where n_t is the period t measure of intermediate goods, is motivated by the fact that society is in possession of a larger stock of knowledge when variety increases. This stock of knowledge should have a positive spillover in the research process. Every generation of researchers should not have to reinvent the wheel, so-to-speak, before creating newer goods. While this is a valid argument, a crucial distinction needs to be made between privately-held knowledge and publicly-held knowledge for this line of reasoning to hold.

The stock of knowledge in the public domain would be accessible at little cost for use in increasing research productivity. However, efforts to obtain sufficient amounts of knowledge privately-held by others and required to increase one's own research productivity would tend to be prohibitively expensive. Essentially, if the required knowledge was not in the public domain, the wheel would have to be reinvented each time by all aspiring researchers at great costs.

If output market competition is steep enough, the profits obtained from entering into the production of an intermediate good through the imitation of the knowledge possessed by the existing producer would be insufficient to cover the substantial costs of imitation. In the extreme case of Bertrand competition, as we have seen above, the monopoly would remain unchallenged. As such, knowledge required for the production of a given intermediate good would remain in the hands of very few people even upon the expiration of patent protection.

Incentives for adding onto the pool of public knowledge from privately-held knowledge also do not exist for individuals. In the case of current producers enjoying monopoly rents there would clearly be a strong disincentive to publicize knowledge. Consider now the case of an individual researcher. Even if some knowledge initially held privately by others was obtained, at significant costs, for use in research by such an individual, he would not have any incentives to subsequently pass such knowledge onto the public domain. Such knowledge would then not be easily available for subsequent generations of researchers either.

Essentially, privately-held knowledge would continue to remain in the private domain and would not be able to contribute to a permanently increased research productivity. As long as knowledge-creation is undertaken in the private sector, such knowledge would, at some point, have to be disseminated and brought into the public realm for it to permanently increase research productivity.

A governmental role in disseminating previously created knowledge is, therefore vital in order to have sustained economic growth. Note that a governmental role is called for *because* of the public good nature of knowledge and the intertemporal increasing returns, from a societal viewpoint, of investment in knowledge creation and not because of the absence or weakness of knowledge spillovers. Essentially, a governmental role is called for because the stock of publicly-held knowledge would tend to increase research productivity forever; however, private incentives to add to this stock by publicizing privately created and held knowledge are absent.

Government can and does increase productivity by publishing and disseminating new knowledge. The agricultural extension program in the United States and efforts by the Japanese government to disseminate existing production technologies among small producers are examples of such efforts. Government subsidies to education and to the public broadcast and printing of educational information are additional examples of a more direct form of dissemination of such knowledge. Section 4 of this chapter addresses the issue of how strong such governmental efforts should be and what their impact on the growth rate of the economy is likely to be.

3.3.2 Savings and the Persistence of Monopoly

When the acquisition of knowledge previously created is costly, monopoly power tends to persist as we have seen. The perpetual monopoly power of producers of intermediate goods rests on the fact that they alone have the knowledge embodied in blueprints for the production of that good. However, once the government effectively brings the private cost of such acquisition to zero by public dissemination of the knowledge, the monopoly power of the holder of the blueprint vanishes at the end of the patent protection period. Otherwise it will last forever.

Such dissemination by government will, as demonstrated below, further contribute to the growth process by diverting savings towards the creation of new goods rather than the purchase of old blueprints. Thus, government has an incentive to disseminate knowledge apart from reasons of increasing productivity in research.

To examine this incentive, let us assume that government can costlessly disseminate knowledge; however, no agent chooses to acquire such knowledge himself. To abstract from the issues raised in section 3.3.1 and to focus on the growth effects of monopoly destruction, we will assume here that an initial dissemination by the government of some of the knowledge in the patent occurs at the time when the good embodying the new knowledge first gets produced. This, therefore, contributes to the research productivity of workers immediately. However, the use of the knowledge in production is barred by patent laws for one period. After the patent expires, the government disseminates the remaining information in the patent that has the effect of destroying monopoly power. The date at which the government chooses to engage in this second dissemination is random for each good. Thus the expected value of each patent is the same.

Under these assumptions, the asset market clearing condition (3.13) has the following form:

$$\delta w_t = x_t w_t + (n_t - m_{t+1})V_t$$

where $m_{t+1} < n_t$ is the measure of goods whose monopoly power has expired. Savings of the young then go towards either the wages of research workers engaged in creating new goods or to the purchase from the old of goods that retain monopoly power. If governmental dissemination of all the knowledge in the patent did not occur, then m_{t+1} would equal zero. As is immediately apparent from the above equation, a lesser amount of the young's savings go towards the purchase of existing monopolies when m_{t+1} is positive. Since the value of patents is given by $V_t = w_t / \lambda n_n$ and research labor by $x_t = \Delta n_{t+1} / \lambda n_t$, substituting these in the above, we have:

$$\lambda \delta + \frac{m_{t+1}}{n_t} = \frac{n_{t+1}}{n_t}$$

Thus the growth rate of variety:

$$\frac{n_{t+1}}{n_t},$$

the direct source of economic growth, is also higher when monopoly power is destroyed; i.e. when $m_{t+1} > 0$.

3.4 PUBLIC DISSEMINATION

Given that the dissemination of knowledge embodied in blueprints and vital for sustained growth is costly, this section examines how a government's choice of effort at publicizing knowledge affects the growth of variety and hence of output.

We will change the assumptions of the model of section I to allow for productivity in research to be affected by only the amount of knowledge that has become disseminated, or is in the public domain, in the economy. Research firms in period t therefore solve the following problem:

$$\max \left(n_{t+1} - n_t\right)V_t - w_t x_t$$

$$\text{s.t.} \quad \Delta n_{t+1} = \lambda h_t x_t,$$

where as before n_t is the measure of intermediate goods in existence in period t, and therefore $(n_{t+1} - n_t)$ is the measure of new intermediate good blueprints created by the x_t units of labor hired for research. V_t is now the *expected* value of a newly created blueprint in period t. As the stream of monopoly profits will end at a random date in the future--a date determined by the government's random choice for the of dissemination of the knowledge inherent in the new blueprint--the expected value of a new blueprint is itself random. Labor's productivity in research increases with the stock of knowledge commonly available: h_t, which is determined by the dissemination process. Due to free entry into research, the profit of the research firm is again driven to zero and the expected value of the patent of a new good is given by:

$$V_t = \frac{w_t}{\lambda h_t}. \tag{3.21}$$

We will assume that for at least one period, the knowledge inherent in the blueprint will not be disseminated. Therefore, there are monopoly profits to be made for at least one period upon successful creation of a new good.

There are now two kinds of intermediate good producers-- those that still retain monopoly power because their knowledge is public, and those that do not possess monopoly power anymore. The former group charges a price above marginal cost,

$$P_t(i) = \frac{w_t}{\alpha},$$

whereas due to Bertrand competition, the price charged by the latter is exactly equal to marginal cost which equals the wage rate. The total wage bill plus profits of the monopolist intermediate good producer is given by:

$$w_t l_t(i) + \pi_t(i) = y_t \cdot \left[\frac{w_t}{\alpha} \right]^{\frac{\alpha}{(\alpha-1)}} \qquad (3.22)$$

and of the competitive producers by:

$$w_t l_t(i) + \pi_t(i) = w_t l_t(i) + 0 = y_t \cdot \left[w_t \right]^{\frac{\alpha}{(\alpha-1)}} \qquad (3.23)$$

Let us denote the measure of monopoly good producers at time t by m_t. The measure of perfectly competitive intermediate good producers is then $(n_t - m_t)$.

Since there are two prices for intermediate goods, the unit cost (normalized to one) of the final good producers is given by:

$$\int_0^{n_t} P_t^{\alpha/(\alpha-1)}(i) \, di = m_t w_t^{\alpha/(\alpha-1)} + (n_t - m_t) z^\alpha w_t^{\alpha/(\alpha-1)} = 1 \qquad (3.24)$$

where

$$z = \frac{1}{\alpha - 1},$$

reflects the constant markup over cost charged by the monopolists.

Using the output decisions of the intermediate good producers, the ratio of output and hence of labor hired between competitive and monopolist producers is:

$$\frac{Q_i^{p.c.}}{Q_i^m} = \frac{l_i^{p.c.}}{l_i^m} = \frac{y_i w_i^{\frac{1}{(\alpha-1)}}}{y_i w_i^{\frac{1}{(\alpha-1)}} z}, \tag{3.25}$$

where p.c. and m. denote perfect competitor and monopolist, respectively.

Integrating (3.22) over the set of all monopolist producers and (3.23) over the set of competitive producers and using (3.24) and (3.25), we obtain:

$$y_t = \left[m_t + z(n_t - m_t) \right] w_t l_t^{p.c} + (n_t - m_t)\pi_t, \tag{3.26}$$

which states that the value of final output has to equal total factor costs plus profits of the intermediate good producers.

Consumer-workers again work in youth and in old age live off the returns to assets previously saved. These assets are in the form of claims to blueprints for the production of intermediate goods. The old then receive the profits of the monopolist firms as dividends and sell their claims to blueprints to the young. The dividend that the old receive is: $(n_t - m_t)\pi_t$, the measure of monopolist intermediate good producers multiplied by the profit. However, during period t, a fraction of the preexisting monopolists lose their market power due to the dissemination of their proprietary knowledge. The size of this fraction is given by: $(m_{t+1} - m_t)$. We assume that it takes at least one period between when knowledge becomes disseminated and when the relevant monopolist loses market power. The claims to the blueprints of these goods becomes worthless as their profits will be driven to zero in the following period. The total consumption of the old is then given by:

$$C_t^{t-1} = (n_t - m_{t+1})V_t + (n_t - m_t)\pi_t \tag{3.27}$$

The consumption of the young is given by:

$$C_t^t = (1 - \tau_t)w_t - S_t, \tag{3.28}$$

where τ_t is the marginal tax rate on wage income and S_t is savings. Using (3.26) and the consumption decisions of the two generations, the output market clearing condition in period t:

$$y_t = C_t^{t-1} + C_t^t$$

can be expressed as:

$$\left[m_t + z(n_t - m_t)\right]w_t l_t^{p.c} + (n_t - m_t)\pi_t$$

$$= (n_t - m_{t+1})V_t + (n_t - m_t)\pi_t + (1 - \tau_t)w_t - S_t \qquad (3.29)$$

The government uses the tax revenue to spread new knowledge. We assume that labor is needed to publicize the knowledge and therefore the tax revenue finances the wages of public employees engaged in the dissemination process. The process through which newly discovered and hence privately-held knowledge is converted into usable form in increasing research productivity is as follows:

$$h_{t+1} = h_t + f(I_t)\left[n_t - m_t\right]; \qquad (3.30)$$

$$f(0) = 0, \quad f(1) < 1,$$

$$f' > 0, \quad f'' < 0.$$

where I_t is labor employed by the government in the dissemination of knowledge. Note that the larger the set of monopoly goods: $\left[n_t - m_t\right]$, the larger the amount of knowledge that is available but not yet in the public domain. Hence, with our functional form for the dissemination process, the increment to public knowledge increases with n_t for a given amount of effort and a given existing base of public knowledge, m_t. This is meant to capture the externality played by knowledge in the dissemination process itself. Given the size of the labor force, we also postulate that it is impossible to publicize the entire stock of knowledge available. Particular innovations whose knowledge is to be disseminated are then chosen randomly.

Given the government's budget constraint:

$$I_t w_t = \tau_t w_t,$$

the fraction of labor employed by the government is exactly equal to the wage tax rate. We will also assume that

$$m_{t+1} = \mu h_t; \quad \mu < 1,$$

i.e. that knowledge made public does not necessarily result in the loss of monopoly power. μ is to be interpreted as the effectiveness of knowledge dissemination in eroding monopoly power. We postulate this in order to isolate and study the impact of dissemination on economic growth via the process of monopoly destruction.

Substituting in the government's budget constraint, (3.21) and the labor constraint:

$$\left[m_t + z(n_t - m_t) \right] w_t l_t^{p.c} + x_t + I_t = 1,$$

into (3.30) we obtain:

$$S_t = \delta(1 - \tau_t) w_t = x_t w_t + \frac{(n_t - m_{t+1})}{\lambda h_t} w_t.$$

Finally, substituting in

$$\Delta n_{t+1} \Big/ \lambda h_t = x_t,$$

we have:

$$\delta(1 - \tau_t) \lambda h_t = n_{t+1} - m_{t+1} \tag{3.31}$$

As can be seen, given m_t, the larger the stock of knowledge that is public (h_t), the larger the set of intermediate goods will be in the following period. This is because research productivity will be higher and thus more new goods will be created. Similarly, the larger the set of existing goods that do not retain monopoly power (m_{t+1}), the larger the set of intermediate goods the following period. This is because the savings of the young will be diverted towards the creation of new goods rather than the purchase of existing blueprints. In their model Chou and Shy assume monopoly power disappears as soon as the patent period is over. We argue that larger efforts are needed than this in order to dilute such power. In either case, if monopoly persists, it causes "crowding out" as identified by Chou and Shy and results essentially in a transfer of income to the old. This transfer retards the growth process as identified by Jones and Manuelli.

The two incentives of the government to publicize knowledge are represented by the variables (h_t) and (m_{t+1}). The cost of increasing the magnitudes of these variables and, thereby, of the number of goods is, however, represented by τ. The choice of optimum τ will be discussed next.

3.5 OPTIMAL DISSEMINATION

The economy is characterized by the following three equations:

$$h_{t+1} = h_t + f(\tau_t)\big[n_t - m_t\big] \qquad (3.32)$$

$$\delta(1 - \tau_t)\lambda h_t = n_{t+1} - m_{t+1} \qquad (3.33)$$

$$m_{t+1} = \mu h_t \qquad (3.34)$$

The first equation is the law of motion for the stock of knowledge that is freely accessible and contributes to research productivity. The second is the asset market clearing condition that relates the number of intermediate goods that will be in existence in the following period to the number of intermediate goods that have lost monopoly power then and the current stock of knowledge. Finally, the last equation states the relationship between the number of monopolies that have lost market power due to dissemination of their knowledge and the stock of disseminated knowledge. τ_t is the marginal tax rate on the young's wage income, or equivalently, the fraction of the labor force employed in the dissemination of knowledge.

We will confine ourselves to a constant tax rate, i.e. $\tau_t = \tau; \quad \forall t$. Lagging (3.33) by one period and substituting it into (3.32), we obtain:

$$h_{t+1} = h_t + f(\tau)\big[\delta(1 - \tau)\lambda h_{t-1}\big],$$

a second order difference equation in the stock of knowledge available to contribute to research productivity. We will look for a balanced growth path in the stock of knowledge, i.e. a steady state in the growth rate of the stock of available knowledge. Defining

$$\hat{h} = h_{t+1}/h_t,$$

the steady state growth rate, we obtain:

$$\hat{h}(\hat{h} - 1) = f(\tau)[\delta\lambda(1 - \tau)] \qquad (3.35)$$

that relates the growth rate of the stock of knowledge to the savings rate δ, a measure of the research productivity of labor independent of the stock of publicly-held knowledge, λ, and the fraction of labor employed in dissemination, or equivalently the tax rate, τ.

Substituting (3.34) into (3.32), we obtain:

$$n_{t+1} = [\mu + \delta\lambda(1 - \tau)]h_t \qquad (3.36)$$

The steady state growth rates of the measure of intermediate goods and of goods that have lost monopoly power are then:

$$\frac{n_{t+1}}{n_t} = \frac{m_{t+1}}{m_t} = \frac{h_{t+1}}{h_t} = 1 + \gamma(\tau, \delta, \lambda). \qquad (3.37)$$

where γ is the growth rate of variety implicitly defined by (3.35).

From (3.36) and (3.34), we also see that the number of intermediate goods that have lost monopoly power by period t, m_t, is a constant proportion of the number of intermediate goods in existence, i.e. $m_t = an_t$, where a is the constant of proportionality:

Consider now, aggregate output.

$$y_t \quad = \left[\int_0^{n_t} Q_t^\alpha (i) \, di \right]^{1/\alpha}$$

$$= \left[m_t + (n_t - m_t)z^\alpha \right]^{1/\alpha} l_t^{pc} \qquad (3.38)$$

where l_t^{pc} is labor hired per non-monopolistic intermediate good. Total labor in production, research and dissemination has to equal one, the size of the labor force.

$$\left[m_t + z(n_t - m_t)\right]l_t^{pc} + x_t + \tau = 1 \qquad (3.39)$$

Total labor in research is, however,

$$x_t = \frac{n_{t+1} - n_t}{\lambda h_t} = \frac{(1+\gamma)n_t}{\lambda \binom{h_t}{\mu}m_t} = \frac{\mu(1+\gamma)}{\lambda a}, \qquad (3.40)$$

where γ denotes the implicitly defined steady state growth rate of h_t, i.e. $h_{t+1} = (1+\gamma)h_t$

Using (3.39), (3.40), and the fact that $m_t = an_t$, (3.38) can be expressed as:

$$y_t = m_t^{(1-\alpha)/\alpha} \frac{\left[1 + \left(\frac{1}{a} - 1\right)z^\alpha\right]^{1/\alpha}\left[1 - \tau - \frac{\mu(1+\gamma)}{\lambda a}\right]}{\left[1 + \left(\frac{1}{a} - 1\right)z\right]} \qquad (3.41)$$

from which we obtain the steady state growth rate of output:

$$\frac{y_{t+1}}{y_t} = \left(\frac{m_{t+1}}{m_t}\right)^{(1-\alpha)/\alpha} = \left(\hat{h}\right)^{(1-\alpha)/\alpha} = \left[1 + \gamma(\tau, \delta, \lambda)\right] \qquad (3.42)$$

The steady state growth rate of output is then a function of the steady state growth rate of publicly-held knowledge, h_t. Setting the derivative of (3.42) with respect to τ equal to zero and using (3.35), we obtain the tax rate that maximizes growth:

$$\frac{\partial y}{\partial \tau} = \left((1-\alpha)/\alpha\right)\hat{h}^{(1-2\alpha)/\alpha} \frac{\delta\lambda}{2\hat{h}-1}\left[(1-\tau)f'(\tau) - f(\tau)\right] = 0 \qquad (3.43)$$

An immediate implication of the above is that the *optimal* (in terms of growth) tax rate is the one that maximizes the growth rate of publicly-held knowledge: $\hat{h}$. This tax rate is furthermore independent of the savings rate: δ, and the "independent" productivity of labor in research, λ. It only depends on the functional form relating the labor employed by the government to success in publicizing privately-held knowledge:

$$f(\tau) = \frac{h_{t+1} - h_t}{n_t - m_t}$$

However, the larger δ and λ are, the larger the growth rate of aggregate output at every tax rate, including at the optimum. This is apparent from differentiating (3.35) totally with respect to each one of these variables to obtain that the growth rate of the stock of publicly - held knowledge: $\hat{h}$, is an increasing function of these variables.

Differentiating (3.43) totally with respect to the tax rate verifies that the second order condition is satisfied. We thus have a unique interior tax rate that maximizes the rate of economic growth. This rate of growth is positively affected by the savings rate and λ .

Note that the effectiveness of increased dissemination of knowledge in affecting output through the destruction of monopoly power is summarized by (3.36). For a given stock of disseminated knowledge, the larger μ --the effectiveness of knowledge in destroying monopoly power--the larger is the extent of intermediate good variety. This is because, more labor will be engaged in research, as is evident from (3.40).

It is instructive to think of two extreme cases. The first is costless dissemination. The optimal amount of dissemination then would clearly be to publicize all the knowledge immediately, i.e. $h_t = n_t$. In this case, the growth rate of variety is given by (3.33) and (3.34):

$$\frac{n_{t+1}}{n_t} = \mu + \delta\lambda .$$

The growth rate of output is $\dfrac{y_{t+1}}{y_t} = \left(\mu + \delta\lambda\right)^{(1-\alpha)/\alpha} .$

Both output and variety are then positively related to the effectiveness with which knowledge destroys monopoly power.

The other extreme case is where dissemination of knowledge contributes to current research productivity immediately and completely destroys monopoly power in the following period, i.e. $\mu = 1$. In this case, the market clearing condition, (3.33), takes the following form:

$$\delta\lambda(1-\tau)m_{t+1} = n_{t+1} - m_{t+1}$$

which in conjunction with the equation of the evolution of knowledge,

$$m_{t+1} = m_t + f(\tau)[n_t - m_t]$$

gives us exactly the same optimal (growth rate maximizing) tax rate as with our original assumptions. In this case, the distinction between the manner in which growth is affected through higher productivity and through a decrease in monopoly power is indistinguishable.

The above two extreme examples highlight the fact that the contribution of more disseminated knowledge in increasing economic growth through the destruction of monopoly power is important. However, the choice of policy variables designed to use this channel depends on the exact manner in which knowledge destroys monopoly power. Furthermore, we have looked at an economy where there is no idiosyncratic risk. Therefore the negative impact on the incentive to conduct research, of a higher risk of losing monopoly power, is not an issue. This impact would, however, need to be examined in more detail to further our understandings of the costs and benefits of public dissemination of knowledge.

3.6 CONCLUDING REMARKS

Future work would best be useful if focused on the microeconomic nature of the dissemination process where labor employed by the government publicizes knowledge. The exact nature of this process is likely to be an important variable in determining the optimal intensity of attempts at diffusion.

The relationship between the dissemination of new knowledge and the dilution of monopoly power also deserves further examination. We have focused on an extreme case where knowledge succeeds in either eroding monopoly power completely or has no effect at all. An examination of the middle ground between these two extremes would be useful.

Finally, the risk of losing monopoly power can be included in the model to examine how such risks affect the intensity of innovation. By adding this possible negative effect of knowledge diffusion, a clearer understanding of the costs and benefits of dissemination could be obtained.

Appendix

A1. TECHNICAL APPENDIX

Derivation of the expected operating profit (chapter I):

Consider the following transformation of the innovation in TFP:

$$u_t^s(i) = \left[1 - \frac{1}{\gamma_t^s(i)}\right]$$

The firm's profit, (1.3), then becomes:

$$u_t^s(i)I_t, \text{ iff } u_t^s(i) > u_t^{s'}(i); \forall s \neq s'; \qquad 0 \text{ otherwise.}$$

The distribution of u is given by: $G(u,x) = \left[\frac{u}{\overline{u}}\right]^{\lambda x}; \overline{u} = \left[1 - \frac{1}{\gamma}\right].$

$$\text{Let } z = \max\left(u^{s'}\right), \forall s' \neq s,$$

i.e. the largest innovation among the competitors of firm s. Then,

$$\Pr[z < \hat{z}] = \Pr\left[\left(u^1 < \hat{z}\right) \cap \ldots \cap \left(u^{s-1} < \hat{z}\right) \cap \left(u^{s+1} < \hat{z}\right) \cap \ldots \cap \left(u^{n-1} < \hat{z}\right)\right]$$

$$= \prod_{s' \neq s} \left[\frac{\hat{z}}{\overline{u}}\right]^{\lambda x^{s'}} = \left[\frac{\hat{z}}{\overline{u}}\right]^{\lambda a}; \text{ where } a = \sum_{s' \neq s} x^{s'}$$

Thus if the variable labor input into research aimed at a given product by firm s is given by x and total variable labor effort by all rivals that engaged in stage I by a, expected profit in period t from this product line for firm s is:

$$= I_t \int_0^{\bar{u}} \int_{\hat{z}}^{\bar{u}} u \, d\left[\left(\frac{u}{\bar{u}}\right)^{\lambda x}\right] d\left[\left(\frac{\hat{z}}{\bar{u}}\right)^{\lambda a}\right]$$

$$= \left[1 - \frac{1}{\gamma}\right] \frac{\lambda x}{\lambda x + \lambda a + 1} \cdot I_t$$

Proof of Proposition II (chapter I):

The first order condition of the problem is:

$$\left[1 - \frac{1}{\gamma}\right] \frac{\lambda(\lambda a_{(i)} + 1)}{(\lambda x^s{}_{(i)} + \lambda a_{(i)} + 1)^2} \cdot \frac{I_t}{R_t w_{t-1}} - 1 = 0.$$

It is easily verified that the second order condition is satisfied. Since we are looking for the equilibrium in a particular product line, we will suppress the dependence of the variables on i. From the first order condition we derive a reaction function for firm s:

$$\hat{x}^s = r(a, v_t),$$

where $$v_t = \frac{I_t}{R_t w_{t-1}}.$$

Suppose firm s is facing $m = n$-1 competitors, the symmetric equilibrium choice of labor intensity targeted at a particular good per firm is then $x^*{}_{(m, v_t)}$ implicitly defined by the reaction function. Also from the F.O.C:

$$\left[1 - \frac{1}{\gamma}\right] \frac{\lambda(\lambda a_{(i)} + 1)}{(\lambda x^s{}_{(i)} + \lambda a_{(i)} + 1)^2} \cdot \frac{I_t}{R_t w_{t-1}} - 1 = 0.$$

Replacing this in (1.4), profit from research can be expressed as:

$$\Pi^*_{(m,v_t)} = w_{t-1}x^* \frac{\lambda x^*}{m\lambda x^* + 1} > 0, \forall m \geq 0 \qquad \text{(A.1)}$$

Replacing the reaction function in the first order condition and totally differentiating with respect to a, we obtain:

$$\frac{\partial}{\partial a} r(a, v_t) = \frac{\lambda x - \lambda a - 1}{2(\lambda a + 1)}.$$

In a symmetric equilibrium with at least two firms $a \geq x$ and so *in equilibrium*, the reaction function is downward sloping. The Nash solution is implicitly defined by:

$$x^* = r(mx^*, v_t). \qquad \text{(A.2)}$$

Treating m as a continuous variable and totally differentiating (A.2), we obtain:

$$\frac{\partial x^*}{\partial m} = \frac{x^* \cdot \frac{\partial r}{\partial a}}{1 - m\frac{\partial r}{\partial a}} < 0.$$

Similarly totally differentiating the Nash profit (A.1) with respect to m, we have:

$$\frac{\partial \Pi^*}{\partial m} = \lambda w_{t-1} \frac{(m\lambda x^{*2} + 2x^*)\frac{\partial x^*}{\partial m} - \lambda x^{*3}}{(m\lambda x^* + 1)^2} < 0.$$

Now consider the effect of v on equilibrium research efforts and profits from research. Totally differentiation (A.2) with respect to v_t,

we obtain:

$$\frac{\frac{\partial r}{\partial v_t}}{1 - m\frac{\partial r}{\partial a}} > 0$$

Totally differentiation (A.1) with respect to I_t, we obtain:

$$\frac{\partial \Pi^*}{\partial I_t} = \lambda w_{t-1} \frac{m\lambda x^{*2} + 2x^*}{\left(m\lambda x^* + 1\right)^2} \frac{\partial x^*}{\partial v_t} \frac{\partial v_t}{\partial I_t} > 0 \text{, and since}$$

$$\frac{\partial \Pi^*}{\partial I_t} = \frac{\partial \Pi^*}{\partial v_t} \frac{\partial v_t}{\partial I_t},$$

we have, $\dfrac{\partial \Pi^*}{\partial v_t} > 0$

Proof of Proposition III (chapter I):

Consider the firm's problem in period t-1:

$$J_{t-1}(\eta_{t-1}) = \max_{\sigma^s_{t-1}} E_{t-1}\left[\tilde{\Pi}_{t-1} - w_{t-1}\bar{x}\right] + J_t(\eta_t)$$

where $\sigma^s_{t-1} \in \left\langle [0,1] \times \left\langle g(\cdot) \right\rangle \times \left\langle h(\cdot) \right\rangle \right\rangle;$

with $g:[0,1] \to R_+$ and $h:[0,1] \to \{\text{develop, not develop}\}$.

J is the firm's profit value function, i.e. the present value of the equilibrium stream of operating profits beginning with period t and research costs beginning with period t-1. The first element of σ is the decision regarding entry, the second the decision regarding how much labor to hire for research for each good in the industry and the third the decision concerning development. We assume that the Bertrand outcomes in the output markets are given. Strategies concerning pricing in the output market can easily be incorporated formally in the above if so desired. η is the distribution of state-of-the-art technologies currently being used for production. Suppose starting from period t, all firms including firm s play according to the equilibrium in the period game analyzed in the chapter. Furthermore suppose $J_t(\eta_t)$ is identically equal to zero for any distribution of state-of -the-art technologies in the industry implemented in period t. The problem is then reduced to the stage game analyzed in the chapter and indeed under equilibrium strategies, $J_{t-1}(\eta_{t-1}) = 0 \; \forall \eta_{t-1}$. Therefore the strategies considered in the chapter do constitute Markov-Nash strategies in the infinite horizon game.

Proof of Proposition IV (chapter I):

Total variable research of an individual firm is just the sum, across all product lines in the industry, of research inputs for each product by the firm. Since the measure of product lines in any given industry is unity, the industry-wide input of an individual firm is, by proposition II, seen to be decreasing in competition.

Consider now total research input by all n participating firms in a *particular* product line: nx^*. Differentiating this totally with respect to n, we have:

$$x^* + n\frac{\partial x^*}{\partial n} = x^*\left[1 + \frac{n\frac{\partial r}{\partial a}}{1 - (n-1)\frac{\partial r}{\partial a}}\right]$$

by the result in proposition II.

Simplifying;

$$= x^*\left[1 + \frac{1 + \frac{\partial r}{\partial a}}{1 - (n-1)\frac{\partial r}{\partial a}}\right]$$

Since

$$\frac{\partial r}{\partial a} = \frac{-(n-1)\lambda x^* - 1}{2(n\lambda x^* + 1)} > -1 ;$$

we have that

$$\frac{\partial (nx^*)}{\partial n} > 0$$

Again since industry-wide research input is the sum of research input in each good, the former is also increasing in competition.

With the transformation of the variable denoting the innovation in total factor productivity, the period t expected operating profit of the firm in a particular product-line, i.e. the winner is equal to:

$\hat{u}I_t$, where $\hat{u} = \max\limits_{s=1,...,n} u^s$, and is given by:

$$\int_0^1 ud\left[\left(\tfrac{u}{\hat{u}}\right)^{\lambda nx}\right] = \left[1-\tfrac{1}{\gamma}\right]\cdot\frac{n\lambda x^*}{n\lambda x^*+1}I_t$$

Differentiating totally with respect to n we get:

$$\left[1-\tfrac{1}{\gamma}\right]\cdot\frac{\lambda\dfrac{\partial}{\partial n}(nx^*)}{\left(n\lambda x^*+1\right)^2}I_t > 0$$

Since the industry is composed of a unit measure of product lines, each having the expected profit derived above, aggregate operating profit of the industry in period t is exactly equal to the expected profit in each product line and is therefore also increasing in competition. Each firm, however, wins the innovation game in only $\left(\tfrac{1}{n}\right)$ of the measure of products in the industry. Therefore the period t operating profit of a given firm in the industry is given by:

$$\left[1-\tfrac{1}{\gamma}\right]\cdot\frac{\lambda x^*}{n\lambda x^*+1}I_t$$

Differentiating this we get,

$$\left[1-\tfrac{1}{\gamma}\right]\cdot\lambda\cdot\frac{\dfrac{\partial}{\partial n}x^*-\lambda x^{*2}}{\left(n\lambda x^*+1\right)^2}I_t < 0$$

Now consider the capital demand by the producing firm in a particular product-line in the industry:

$$k_t = \frac{\alpha I_t}{\gamma_t^* R_t} = \frac{\alpha P_t(i) Q_t(i)}{\gamma_t^* R_t},$$

where $\qquad \gamma_t^* = \max_{s=1,\dots,n} \gamma_t^s.$

Using the transformation considered earlier, we get,

$$\frac{R_t k_t}{P_t(i) Q_t(i)} = (1 - \hat{u}) \cdot \alpha.$$

Taking expected value, we have:

$$\mathrm{E}\left[\frac{R_t k_t}{P_t(i) Q_t(i)}\right] = \alpha \cdot \frac{\frac{1}{\bar{\gamma}} \cdot n\lambda x^* + 1}{n\lambda x^* + 1}. \tag{A.3}$$

Finally upon differentiation, we obtain:

$$-\left[\frac{\bar{\gamma}-1}{\bar{\gamma}}\right] \cdot \frac{\lambda \alpha}{\left[n\lambda x^* + 1\right]^2} < 0.$$

Integrating across i, we obtain industry sales to capital cost to be exactly equal to the inverse of (A.3) which is then increasing in competition. The exact same applies for the ratio of industry sales to the cost of production labor.

Proof of Proposition V (chapter II):

We will prove this proposition by using the following property of binomial expectations:

Property1:

$$h(n) \overset{>}{\underset{<}{}} h(n+1) \Rightarrow \frac{\partial}{\partial q}\left[\sum_{n=0}^{N}\binom{N}{n} q^n (1-q)^{N-n} h(n)\right] \overset{<}{\underset{>}{}} 0$$

Proof: Differentiate, collect terms and let $m = n - 1$ to obtain:

$$N\sum_{m=0}^{N-1}\binom{N-1}{m}q^m(1-q)^{N-1-m}\left[h(m+1)-h(m)\right]$$

Now first consider the zero expected profit condition of the firm, equation (1.6) in chapter 1:

$$\Phi_1(q_t,v_{t+1})=\sum_{m=0}^{N-1}\binom{N-1}{m}q_t^m(1-q_t)^{N-1-m}\bullet$$

$$\left[\left[1-\tfrac{1}{\gamma}\right]\frac{\lambda x^*}{(m+1)\lambda x^*+1}\frac{y_{t+1}}{R_{t+1}}-w_t x^*-w_t\bar{x}_{(j)}\right]=0$$

where m is the number of competitors, each of whom engages with probability q, that a particular firm expects to compete in research with once it itself engages in research. The above then is expected profit prior to entry conditional on the firm's own entry and the probability of entry of each one of its N-1 potential competitors. Using the first order condition (derived in chapter 1)

$$\frac{y_t}{R_t}=\frac{w_{t-1}}{\left[1-\tfrac{1}{\gamma}\right]}\cdot\frac{\left[(m+1)\lambda x^*+1\right]^2}{\lambda\left[m\lambda x^*+1\right]},$$

to transform the profit function we obtain

$$\sum_{m=0}^{N-1}\binom{N-1}{m}q_t^m(1-q_t)^{N-1-m}w_t x^*\left[\frac{\lambda x^*}{m\lambda x^*+1}-\bar{x}\right]=0$$

The term,
$$w_{t-1}x^* \frac{\lambda x^*}{m\lambda x^* + 1}$$

was shown to be decreasing in m and increasing in v_t in the proof of proposition II. The right hand side of the above is then clearly increasing in v_{t+1} and by the above property, it is decreasing in q_t. Applying the implicit function theorem to the zero profit condition, we then get:

$$\frac{\partial q_t}{\partial v_{t+1}} > 0.$$

Next consider the asset market clearing condition:

$$\Phi_2(q_t, v_{t+1}) = \frac{\beta}{\beta+1} - \sum_{n=0}^{N} \binom{N}{n} q_t^n (1-q_t)^{N-n} \left[\frac{K_{t+1}^*}{W_t} + L_t^r \right] = 0 \qquad \text{(A.4)}$$

Substituting for total research labor (variable as well as fixed) demanded in period t if n firms engage; and expected capital demanded in period t+1 in a particular product line if n firms engaged in period t (which by the law of large numbers will be equal to the total capital demanded in period t+1 if in each industry n firms engaged) in the above, we obtain.

$$\frac{\beta}{\beta+1} - \sum_{n=0}^{N} \binom{N}{n} q_t^n (1-q_t)^{N-n} \left[\frac{\frac{1}{\gamma} n\lambda x^* + 1}{n\lambda x^* + 1} \alpha v_{t+1} + n\left[x^* + \bar{x}\right] \right] = 0$$

Let
$$g(n, v_{t+1}) = \left[\frac{\frac{1}{\gamma} n\lambda x^* + 1}{n\lambda x^* + 1} \alpha v_{t+1} + n\left[x^* + \bar{x}\right] \right].$$

Differentiating $g(\cdot)$ with respect to n, we obtain:

$$\frac{\partial}{\partial n}\left[nx^*\right] \cdot \left[1 - \frac{\frac{\gamma-1}{\gamma}\lambda\alpha v_{t+1}}{\left[n\lambda x^* + 1\right]^2} \right].$$

Substituting from the first-order-condition of the firm and rearranging:

$$\frac{\partial}{\partial n}\left[nx^*\right]\cdot\left[1-\frac{\alpha}{\left[(n-1)\lambda x^*+1\right]}\right]>0$$

by the proof of proposition IV in chapter I where it was shown that

$$\frac{\partial}{\partial n}\left[nx^*\right]>0 \text{ and the fact that } \alpha<1.$$

By property 1, the left hand side of (A.4) is then decreasing in q_t. Similarly differentiating $g(\cdot)$ with respect to v_{t+1}, and using the first-order condition of the firm to rearrange, we obtain:

$$\frac{\frac{1}{\gamma}n\lambda x^*+1}{n\lambda x^*+1}\alpha+\frac{\partial}{\partial n}\left[nx^*\right]\cdot\left[1-\frac{\alpha}{\left[(n-1)\lambda x^*+1\right]}\right]>0$$

Applying the implicit function theorem to (A.4), we then obtain that $\frac{\partial q_t}{\partial v_{t+1}}<0$. Next, let the following be as defined:

$$v_1^1 = v \text{ such that } \Phi_1(0,v)\equiv 0$$
$$v_2^1 = v \text{ such that } \Phi_2(0,v)\equiv 0$$
$$v_1^2 = v \text{ such that } \Phi_1(1,v)\equiv 0$$
$$v_1^2 = v \text{ such that } \Phi_2(1,v)\equiv 0$$

If λ is sufficiently large, we know , $\exists v_t \in (0,\frac{\beta}{(\beta+1)\alpha})$,

an interior solution to the monopolist's problem. Therefore since $\Phi_1(q_t,v_{t+1})$ is increasing in v, for sufficiently small $\overline{x}$,

$$\exists v_1^1 < v_2^1 = \frac{\beta}{(\beta+1)\alpha}.$$

Similarly, because $\Phi_1(q_t,v_{t+1})$ is increasing in v and decreasing in N whereas $\Phi_2(q_t,v_{t+1})$ is increasing in both v and N, $\exists v_1^2 > v_2^2$.

By the intermediate value theorem there then exists a unique pair $(\overline{q}, \overline{v})$ that satisfies both the zero profit condition and the asset market clearing condition.

A2. DATA APPENDIX

Table 1. Firm-Level Observations

Dependent Variable	Constant	Number of Firms
1. OLS		
Industry Profit	-44823	935.028
	(-2.481)	(1.640)
1982 Firm R&D	139.891	-2.30262
	(5.723)	(-2.986)
1982 Industry R&D	1256.98	6.79653
	(3.507)	(0.601)
1983 Firm R&D	142.906	-2.27828
	(5.761)	(-2.911)
1987 Industry	6775.94	-29.9945
Investment	(2.894)	(-0.406)
2. Heteroscedasticity Corrected OLS		
Industry Profit	-44823	935.028
	(-3.752)	(3.434)
1982 Firm R&D	139.891	-2.30262
	(4.022)	(-2.617)
1982 Industry R&D	1256.98	6.79653
	(4.597)	(0.745)
1983 Firm R&D	142.906	-2.27828
	(4.099)	(-2.585)
1987 Industry	6775.94	-29.9945
Investment	(4.036)	(-1.271)

sample size 189; t-statistics in parenthesis.

Table 2. 2-Digit Industry Observations on Capital Services

Independent Variable	Dependent Variables	
	(RK/GDP)	(RK/GDP) Heteroskedasticity Consistent
Constant	4.2060	4.2060
	(6.811)	(5.945)
Number of Firms	-0.04095	-0.04095
	(-2.979)	(-2.590)

sample size 42; t-statistics in parenthesis.

Table 3. 4-Digit Industry Observations on Labor Costs

Independent Variable	Dependent Variables	
	Sales/labor cost OLS	Sales/labor cost Heteroskedasticity Consistent OLS

1. Apparel and Other Textile Products (sample size 99)

Constant	5.344	5.344
	(33.781)	(32.050)
Number of Firms	-0.001	-0.001
	(-0.764)	(-0.630)

2. Textile Mill Products (sample size 81)

Constant	6.549	6.549
	(17.132)	(18.329)
Number of Firms	-0.011	-0.011
	(-1.121)	(-1.453)

Table 3. 4-Digit Industry Observations on Labor Costs (continued)

Independent Variable	Dependent Variables	
	Sales/labor cost	Sales/labor cost Heteroskedasticity
	OLS	Consistent OLS

3. Food and Kindred Products (sample size 132)

Constant	15.322	15.322
	(7.152)	(5.640)
Number of	0.0795	0.0795
Firms	(1.678)	(0.6885)

4. Primary Metal Industries (sample size 66)

Constant	15.598	15.598
	(5.422)	(4.633)
Number of	-0.176	-0.176
Firms	(-2.146)	(-2.838)

5. Chemicals and Allied Products (sample size 63)

Constant	10.371	10.371
	(9.627)	(8.948)
Number of	0.075	0.075
Firms	(1.875)	(2.376)

6. Stone, Clay and Glass Products (sample size 78)

Constant	4.280	4.280
	(21.42)	(20.963)
Number of	0.007	0.007
Firms	(4.991)	(7.911)

t-statistics in parenthesis.

Table 4. 4-Digit Industry Observations on Capital Costs

Independent Variable	Dependent Variables	
	Sales/labor cost	Sales/labor cost Heteroskedasticity Consistent

1. Apparel and Other Textile Products (sample size 99)

Constant	98.014	98.014
	(14.045)	(14.494)
Number of	0.223	0.223
Firms	(4.580)	(3.847)

2. Textile Mill Products (sample size 81)

Constant	45.939	45.939
	(11.623)	(11.625)
Number of	-0.220	-0.220
Firms	(-0.224)	(-0.278)

3. Food and Kindred Products (sample size 132)

Constant	54.309	54.309
	(14.573)	(14.456)
Number of	0.198	0.198
Firms	(0.240)	(0.225)

4. Primary Metal Industries (sample size 66)

Constant	39.498	39.498
	(6.006)	(4.565)
Number of	-0.145	-0.145
Firms	(-0.771)	(-0.800)

Table 4. 4-Digit Industry Observations on Capital Costs (continued)

Independent Variable	Dependent Variables	
	Sales/labor cost	Sales/labor cost Heteroskedasticity Consistent
5. Chemicals and Allied Products (sample size 63)		
Constant	19.461	19.461
	(6.240)	(6.567)
Number of	0.402	0.402
Firms	(3.452)	(3.608)
6. Stone, Clay and Glass Products (sample size 78)		
Constant	34.897	34.897
	(10.759)	(10.334)
Number of	-0.363	-0.036
Firms	(-1.713)	(-3.704)

t-statistics in parenthesis.

Table 5. Growth Rates and Research Personnel: Correlations

	GDP growth (1981-88)	Capital growth (1981-88)	RSE % of Labor Force
GDP growth (1981-88)	1	0.635	0.332
Capital growth (1981-88)		1	0.600
RSE % of Labor Force			1

Source of data: Summers, R. and A. Heston (1991) "The Penn World Table (Mark 5): An Expanded Set of International Comparisons,

1950-1988. *"Quarterly Journal of Economics CVI"*; and OECD (1991): *Basic Science and Technology Statistics.* Paris.

RSE % of labor force is the percentage of the labor force classified as research scientists and engineers and is calculated as the average for the years that data was available between 1981 and 1988. Sample size for gdp growth and capital stock are 22 and 17 countries, respectively. In calculating the correlation between growth of capital and growth of gdp, 5 countries where data for capital stock was unavailable were dropped.

Bibliography

Aghion, P. and P. Howitt. (1992): "A Model of Growth through Creative Destruction." *Econometrica 60, no. 2*, pp. 323-352.

Atkeson, Andrew and Patrick J. Kehoe. (1993): "Industry Evolution and Transition: The Role of Information Capital." Research manuscript.

Chou, C. and O. Shy (1993): "The Crowding-out Effects of Long Duration of Patents." *Rand Journal of Economics*, 24(2), pp.304-312.

Domowitz, I., Hubbard, R. and B. Peterson (1986): "Business Cycles and the Relationship between Concentration and Price-Cost Margins." *Rand Journal of Economics 17, no.1*, pp. 1-17.

Easterlin, R. (1981): "Why Isn't The Whole World Developed ?" *Journal of Economic History*, pp. 1-19.

Freeman, C. (1988): "Japan: A New National System of Innovation ?", in G. Dosi et al. eds. *Technical Change and Economic Theory*. Printer Publishers, New York and London.

Grossman, G. and A. Helpman (1989): "Product Development and International Trade." *Journal of Political Economy*, 97, (Dec), pp. 1261-1283.

_____ (1991a): *Innovation and Growth in the Global Economy*. MIT Press.

_____ (1991b): "Quality Ladders in the Theory of Growth." *Review of Economic Studies 58*, pp.43-61.

Hall, B. and F. Hayashi (1989): "Research and Development as an Investment." NBER Working Paper no. 2973.

Hall, Robert. (1986): "The Relation Between Price and Marginal Cost in U.S. Industry." *Journal of Political Economy 96, no .5*, pp.921-947.

Hart, P.E. (1971): "Entropy and Other Measures of Concentration." *Journal of the Royal Statistical Society*, series A, 134:73-85.

Jones, L. and R. Manuelli (1992): "Finite Lifetimes and Growth." *Journal of Economic Theory 58*, pp.171-197.

Jorgenson, D., Gallop, F., and B. Fraumeni (1987): *Productivity and U.S. Economic Growth*. Cambridge, MA. Harvard University Press.

Jovanovic, B. (1981): "Entry with Private Information." *Bell Journal* 12, no. 2, pp. 649-660.

Judd, K. (1985): "The Law of Large Numbers with a Continuum of IID Random Variables." *Journal of Economic Theory* 35, pp. 19-25.

Lach, S. and Rafael Rob. (1992): "R&D, Investment and Industry Dynamics." CARESS Working Paper. University of Pennsylvania.

Lee, T. and L. Wilde. (1980): "Market Structure and Innovation: A Reformulation." *Quarterly Journal of Economics* XCIV (March), pp. 429-436.

Levin, R. and P. C.Reiss. (1984): "Tests of a Schumpeterian Model of R&D and Market Structure." in *R&D, Patents, and Productivity*, ed. Griliches, Z. University of Chicago Press.

Loury, G. (1979) "Market Structure and Innovation." *Quarterly Journal of Economics* XCIII (Aug), pp. 395-410.

Mansfield, E, M. Schwartz and S. Wagner. (1981): "Imitation Costs and Patents: An Empirical Study." *The Economic Journal, 91* (December), pp. 907-918.

Reinganum, J. (1982): "A Dynamic Game of R&D, Patent Protection and Competitive Behaviour." *Econometrica* L (May), pp. 671-688.

_____ (1985): "Innovation and Industry Evolution." *Quarterly Journal of Economics* C (Feb). pp. 81-100.

Romer, P. (1986): "Increasing Returns and Long Run Growth." *Journal of Political Economy* 94, pp.1002-1037.

_____ (1990a): "Endogenous Technological Change." *Journal of Political Economy*, 98. S71-S102.

_____ (1990b): "Notes of Growth with Multiple Equilibria." Research Paper, Palais du Luxembourg.

Rotemberg, J. and G. Saloner. (1986): "A Supergame-theoretic Model of Business Cycles and Price Wars during Booms." *American Economic Review* 76, vol.3, pp. 390-407.

Rustichini, A. and J. Schmitz (1991): "Research and Imitation and Long-Run Growth." *Journal of Monetary Economics* 27. pp. 271-292.

Scherer, F. (1967): "Market Structure and the Employment of Scientists and Engineers." *American Economic Review* 57, vol. 3. pp. 524-530.

Schumpeter, J. (1934): *The Theory of Economic Development.* New York: Oxford University Press.

_____ (1942): *Capitalism, Socialism and Democracy.* New York: Harper and Brothers.

Scott, J. (1984): "Firm versus Industry Variability in R&D Intensity." *in R&D, Patents, and Productivity*, ed. Griliches, A. University of Chicago Press.

Segerstrom, P., Anant, T. and E. Dinopoulos (1990): "A Schumpeterian Model of the Product Life Cycle." *American Economic Review* 80, pp. 1077-1091.

Tirole, J. (1988): *The Theory of Industrial Organization.* MIT Press.

Uhlig, Harald. (1988): "A Law of Large Numbers for Large Economies." Manuscript.

Uhlig, Harald and Noriyuki Yanagawa. (1992): "Higher Capital Income Taxes Mean Faster Growth." Manuscript, Princeton University.

Index

For Product Safety Concerns and Information please contact our EU
representative GPSR@taylorandfrancis.com Taylor & Francis Verlag GmbH,
Kaufingerstraße 24, 80331 München, Germany

Printed and bound by CPI Group (UK) Ltd, Croydon, CR0 4YY
08/05/2025
01864380-0002